RECORDED VERSIONS
GUITAR

AUTHENTIC TRANSCRIPTIONS
WITH NOTES AND TABLATURE

JONNY LANG
LONG TIME COMING

Cover artwork licensed courtesy of A&M Records
© 2003 A&M Records

Music transcriptions by Pete Billmann

ISBN 0-634-06877-6

HAL•LEONARD®
CORPORATION
7777 W. BLUEMOUND RD. P.O. BOX 13819 MILWAUKEE, WI 53213

Visit Hal Leonard Online at
www.halleonard.com

www.jonnylang.com

Photo by Ashley Johnson

JONNY LANG
LONG TIME COMING
BIOGRAPHY

It's not important where you've been, but where you are, and at 22, Jonny Lang is right where he wants to be. Though his past awards, commendations and achievements are enough – including having two platinum-selling albums and a Grammy nomination by age 19 – Jonny comments, "I'm the happiest I've ever been, and I've just finished recording an album I couldn't be happier with."

That album is the aptly titled *Long Time Coming*. It is Jonny's third release, but it celebrates several noteworthy firsts: this time around he not only wrote or co-wrote all but one of the album's tracks, and served as its co-producer, but also he has made an album that he feels very honestly reflects who he is.

With a four-year gap between his last album and *Long Time Coming*, many people have questioned his whereabouts. Taking it in stride, Jonny revealed his sense of humor and good nature by once joking with an interviewer, "I promise it'll come out before I'm 40." Launching a preemptive strike by naming it *Long Time Coming*, Jonny explains, "Of course the title is about how long it's been since I've had an album out, and it's pretty much about trying to be patient."

Photo by Ashley Johnson

A more fully realized album than his earlier efforts, *Long Time Coming* has a much greater emphasis on the songs than ever before. Jonny channeled an autobiography of sorts into this album. And, as it turns out, Lang has a gift in creating gritty, heartfelt songs about relationships precariously poised on the edge, and winsome love paeans. With the help of co-producer Marti Fredrickson (Ozzy Osbourne, Aerosmith, Faith Hill), he has been able to craft a dozen soulful and canny songs that are full of nuances and emotion, conjuring up a spirit of Muscle Shoals and Motown, filtered down through his own life experiences. "The album is really a journal of my life for the past two years," reveals Jonny.

Initially not feeling up to the task of writing his own songs, after a single day in the studio with Fredrickson he was convinced. "Marti and I got together to do a song and the first song we did was 'Give Me Up Again' and everyone loved it. This album really is all about the songs. To me, I knew I succeeded when I could get them to sound just like you would say them. Like in a conversation. They all seemed to make sense that way."

Marti also helped Jonny develop a new respect for his prodigious talent on guitar. Though the blues guitar great Jimmy Thackery once commented about Lang, "He plays so good, I want to break his fingers," Marti pushed Jonny past his comfort level.

"It really humbled me working with Marti because it was the first time anyone really critiqued my playing," says Jonny. "Before I could just play whatever, solo or whatever, little guitar riffs between vocal lines and be like, 'okay, cool, we'll just keep that.' But when I was in the studio with Marti I'd play something and he'd be like, 'That sucks.

You can do better than that.' Of course I'm getting all offended. But after a while I just really grew to just love him for that because I learned I'm the kind of person who should be produced."

And about the album's first single "Red Light," a cover which he makes his own, Jonny comments "It's rare to cover a song and feel you're really a part of it. There are those times when you feel like you can really relate to the song. And that's what happened with it. It's also great to be able to record a song and have fun doing it."

Working alongside Fredrickson not only allowed Jonny to grow musically, but encouraged some self-exploration as well. "It was incredible how well we worked together. It was pure chemistry," Jonny enthuses. "I felt like he made me more of myself and for the first time, I felt like this is the 'real me.'"

Not without impressive backing, Lang and Fredrickson commissioned the help of a rock and roll great for this much-anticipated release by asking Steven Tyler to contribute to a track. "Steven doesn't sing, but he plays harmonica on 'Happiness and Misery,'" explains Jonny. "He's such a nice guy. He is not a prima donna at all. We asked him to play and he was like, 'Yeah man. Send me the tracks; I'll do it right away.'"

Photo by Ashley Johnson

With age and maturity, Jonny is growing into his vocal gifts. When he began his career at 13 years old, his voice, which sounded aged and weathered, inspired *U.S. News and World Report* to write, "Don't be fooled by that peach-smooth face. Jonny Lang has the voice of a grizzled blues veteran with a 20-year Marlboro habit – and guitar skills to match." But on *Long Time Coming*, there is more of an authentic expression of who he is, passionately veering somewhere between rock and soul.

"This is the most complete thing I've done. I think everything else has been okay up to now," Jonny continues, "On my other albums, I felt I was kind of pigeonholed as doing what a blues guitar player dude should do, but in my mind, I'm not a blues singer. And I'm not a blues writer either. This record is more rock than any of the others, but there are a lot of different things going on in there."

Now when Jonny Lang performs he feels more of a connection to the songs and his audience. "I used to feel when I would sing or play guitar it would all go off into thin air and disappear somewhere. But now it feels like something is happening when I play music. It's not just to satisfy myself, but it's about giving with my music. And that makes all the difference."

Photo by Ashley Johnson

Give Me Up Again

Words and Music by Jonny Lang and Marti Frederiksen

I'd be do - in' fine _____ with or with - out _____ you. _____ I'm

wast - in' my _____ time _____ let - ting you _____ de - ceive _____ me. The

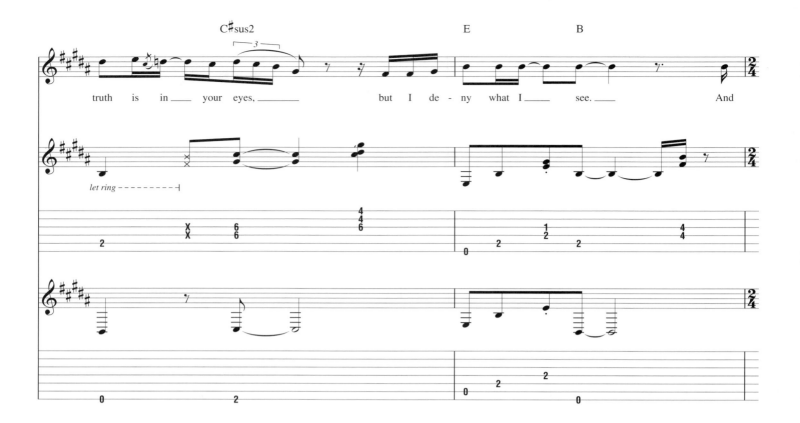

break me down_ a-gain. And I let you in ____ close, way too close,_ but I see through_

_____ it. _____ You gave me that smile and I gave in, ___ and you

knew that I would.   Time and time __ a - gain __ you pulled __ me in   just to give me up, __   give me up __ a - gain. __

End Rhy. Fig. 1

End Rhy. Fig. 1A

Interlude
Gtr. 3 tacet

Yeah. _____

Gtr. 4

w/ fingers ----------------------

Gtr. 2

mp

12

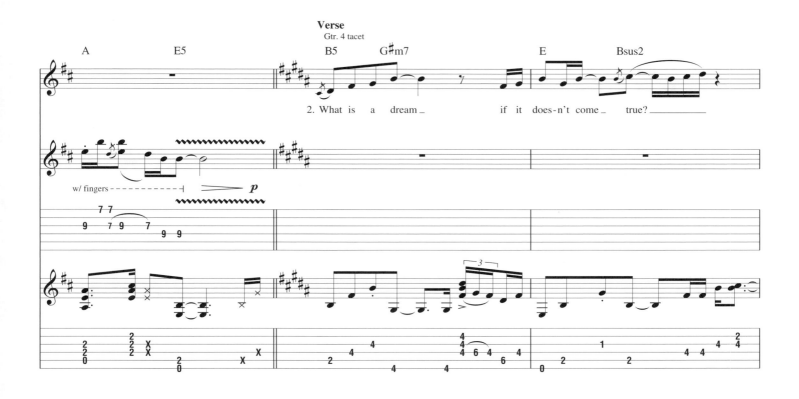

Verse
Gtr. 4 tacet

2. What is a dream _ if it does-n't come _ true? _____

w/ fingers

*Sung behind the beat.

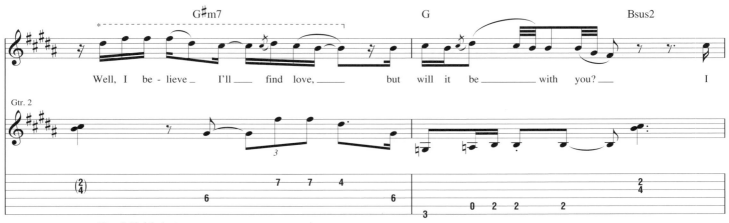

Well, I be - lieve _ I'll _ find love, _____ but will it be _____ with you? _ I

Gtr. 2

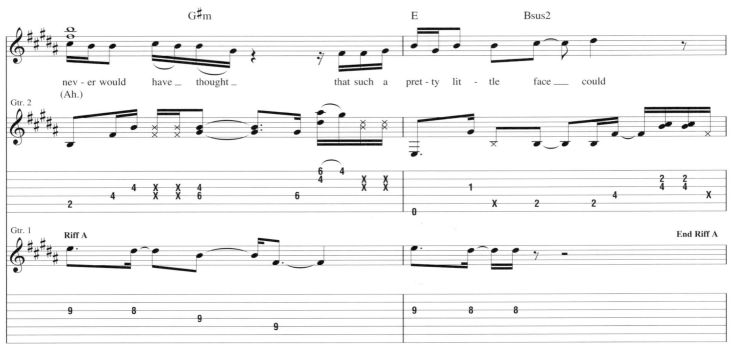

nev - er would have _ thought _____ that such a pret - ty lit - tle face _ could
(Ah.)

Gtr. 2

Gtr. 1
Riff A

End Riff A

14

break me down _ a - gain. _ I let you in _ close, way too close, but I see through _

_ it. _ You gave me that _ smile and I gave in, _ and you

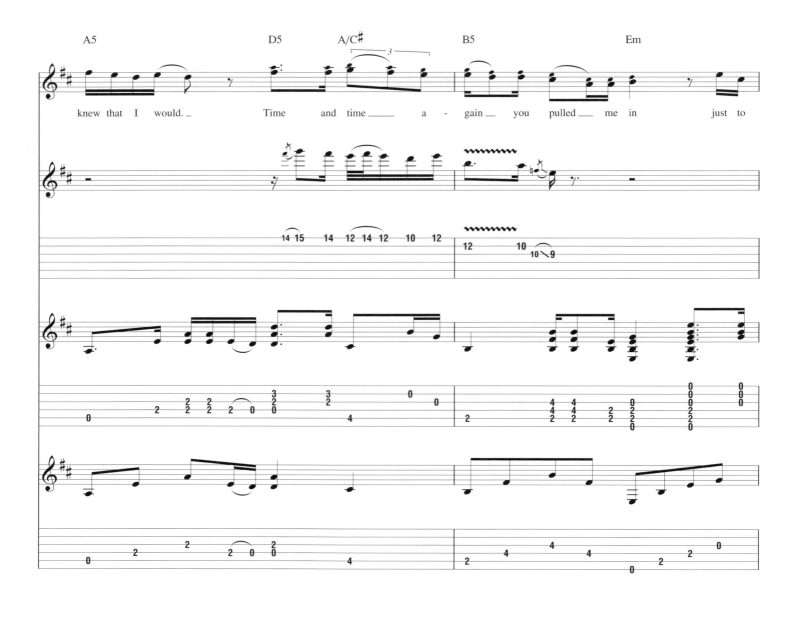

A5   D5   A/C#   B5   Em

knew that I would. _ Time and time _____ a - gain __ you pulled __ me in just to

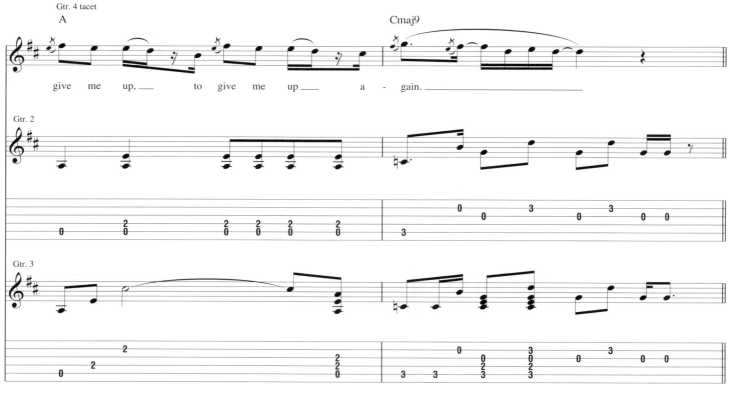

Gtr. 4 tacet

A   Cmaj9

give me up, __ to give me up __ a - gain. _____

Gtr. 2

Gtr. 3

16

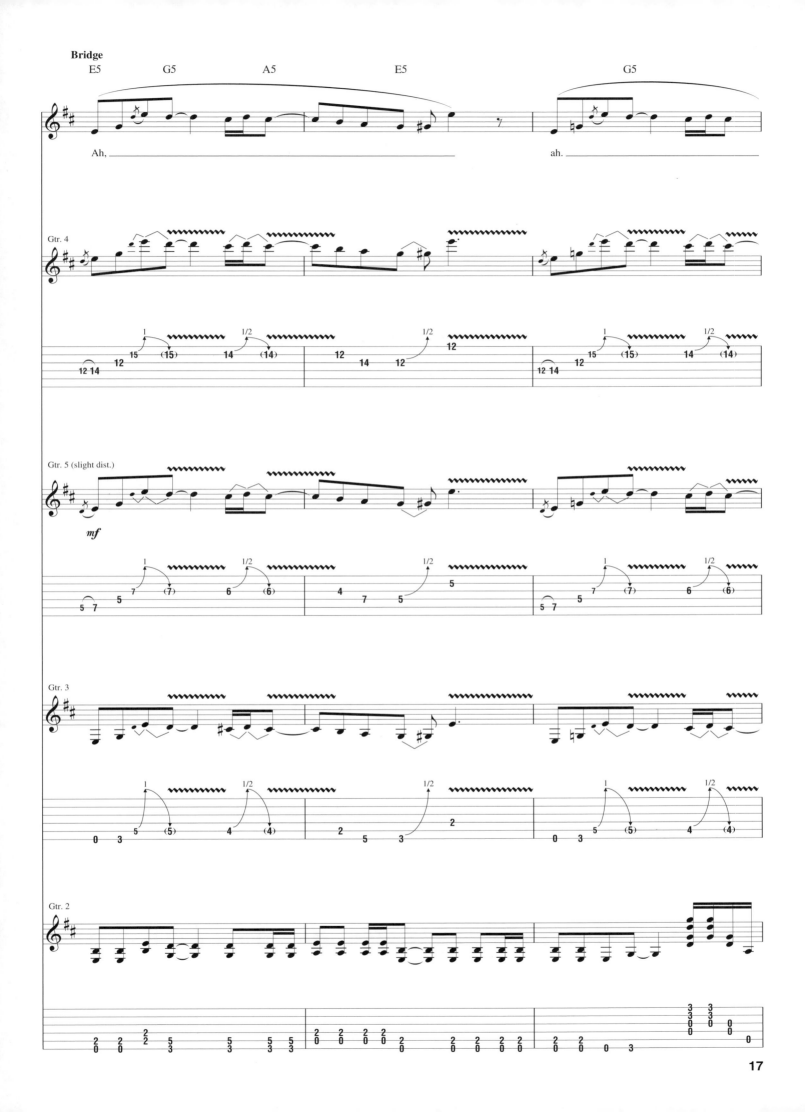

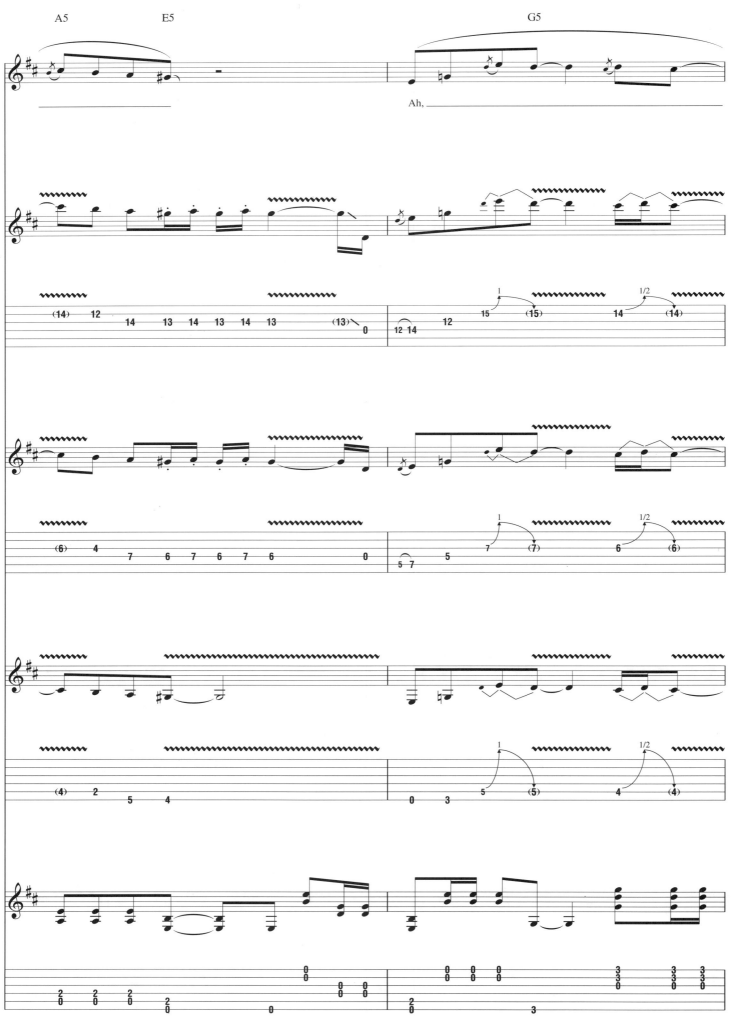

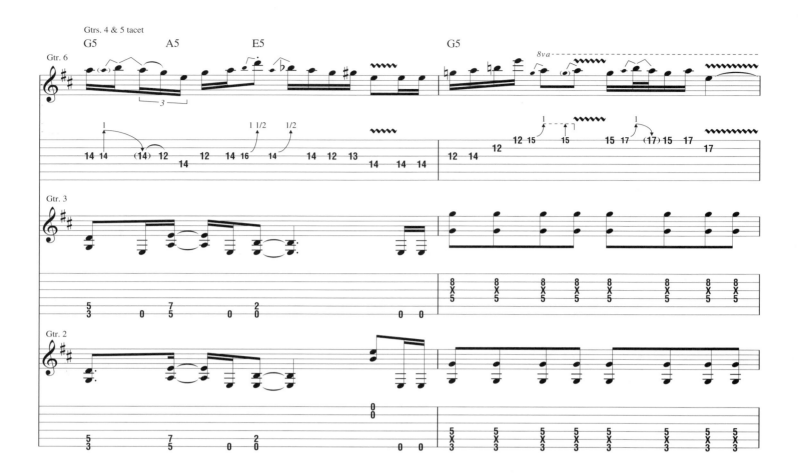

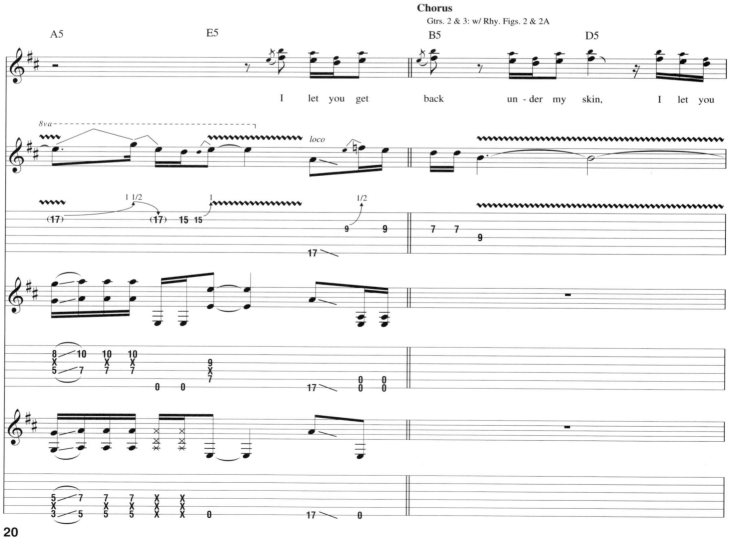

Chorus
Gtrs. 2 & 3: w/ Rhy. Figs. 2 & 2A

I let you get back under my skin, I let you

break me down _ a - gain. _ I let you in close, way too close, _ but I see through _ _ it, _ heh. Once you gave me that smile and I gave in _ and you knew that I would. Time and time _ a - gain _ you pulled _ me in just to give me up, to give me up _ a - gain. _ Oh, _ a - gain. _ Time and time _ a -

gain _ you pulled _ me in   just to give me up, _   give me _ up,   give me up _ a - gain. _

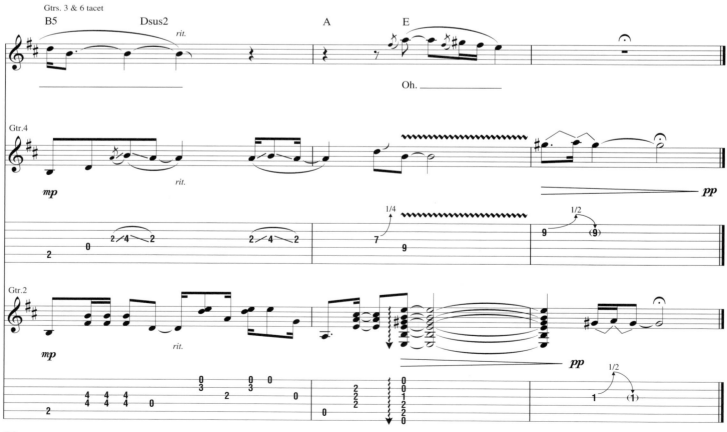

Oh. _____

Red Light

Words and Music by Anthony Cornelius Hamilton and Neely Dinkins, Jr.

Gtrs. 1, 2, 3 & 5: Tune down 1/2 step:
(low to high) E♭-A♭-D♭-G♭-B♭-E♭

Gtr. 4: Drop D tuning, down 1/2 step:
(low to high) D♭-A♭-D♭-G♭-B♭-E♭

Intro
Moderately ♩ = 123
Half-time feel

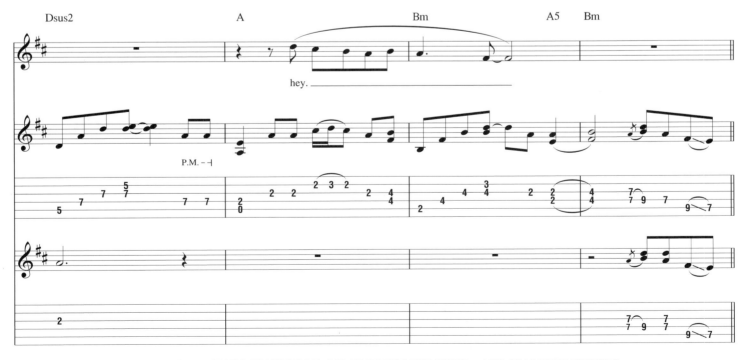

Verse

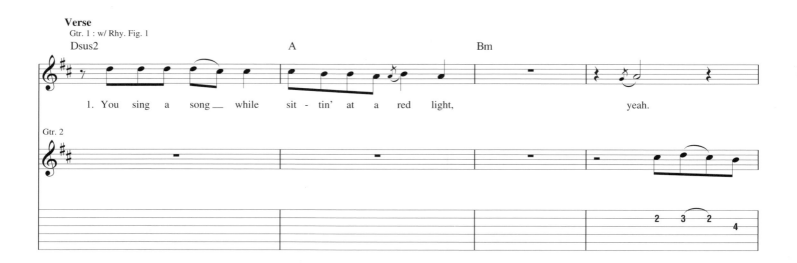

End half-time feel

look low, ___ you've got ___ to keep strong. __ Feet __ to the grass, __ you've got-ta walk it up. The bow's __

__ been tied __ too tight ___ to laugh. __ Feet __ to the ground, __ you've got to walk it off. Oh. __

Guitar Solo

Gtr. 1: w/ Rhy. Fig. 5 (1 1/2 times)
Gtr. 3: w/ Riff B (1 1/2 times)

*Refers to bkgd. voc. only.

(You can run a red ____ light.)

Oh, ____

(You can run a red ____ light.)

End Voc. Fig. 1

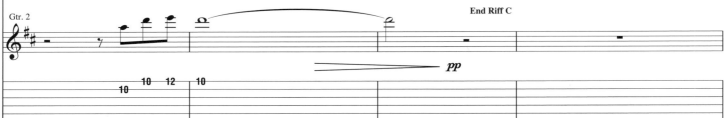

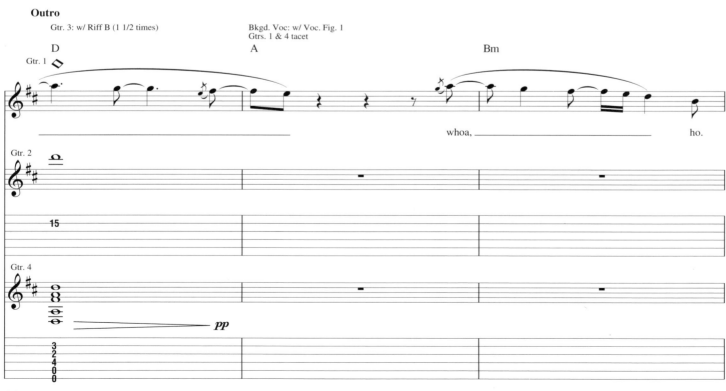

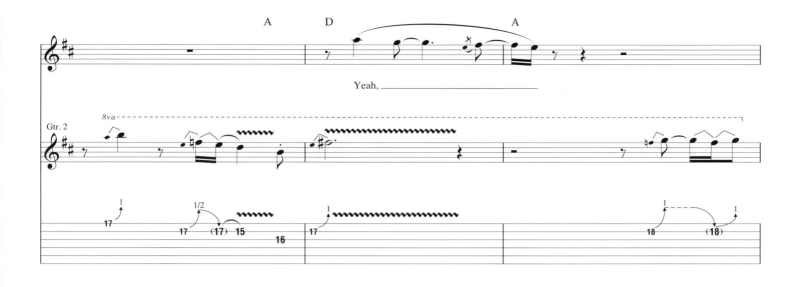

Yeah, _____

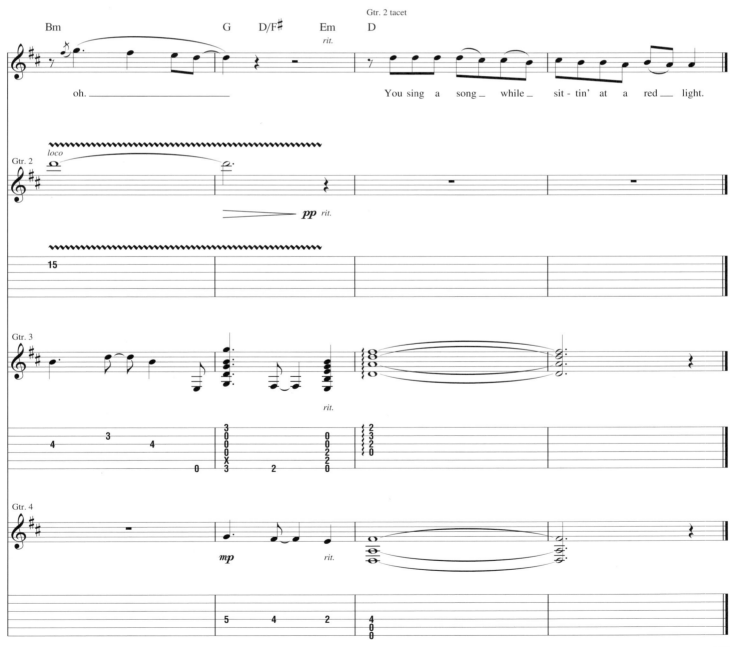

oh. _____

You sing a song_ while_ sit - tin' at a red_ light.

Get What You Give

Words and Music by Jonny Lang and Marti Frederiksen

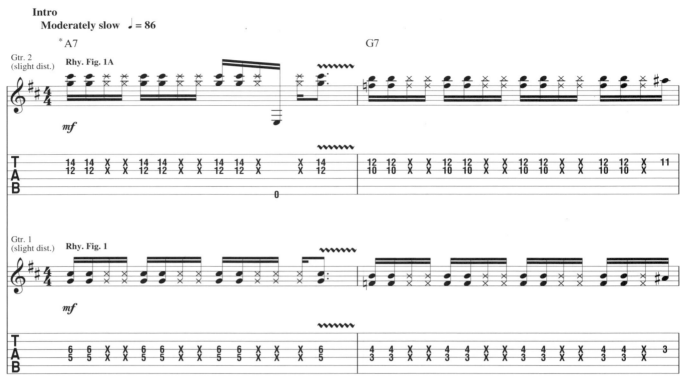

*Chord symbols reflect implied harmony.

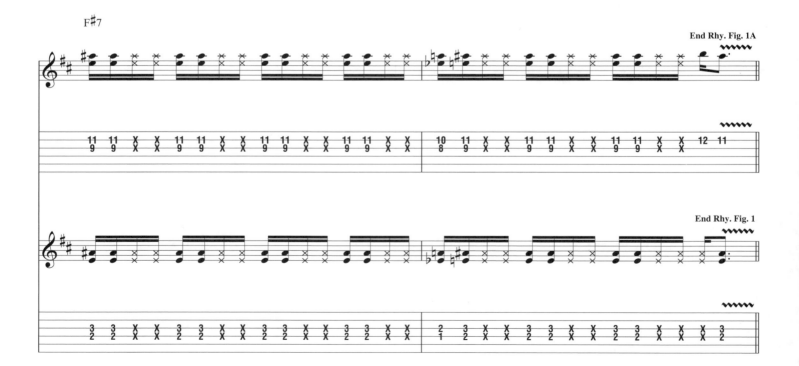

Verse

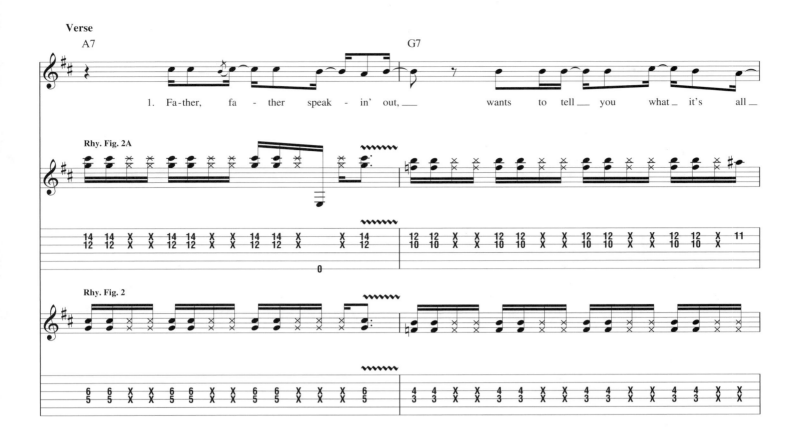

1. Fa-ther, fa - ther speak - in' out, ___ wants to tell ___ you what ___ it's all ___

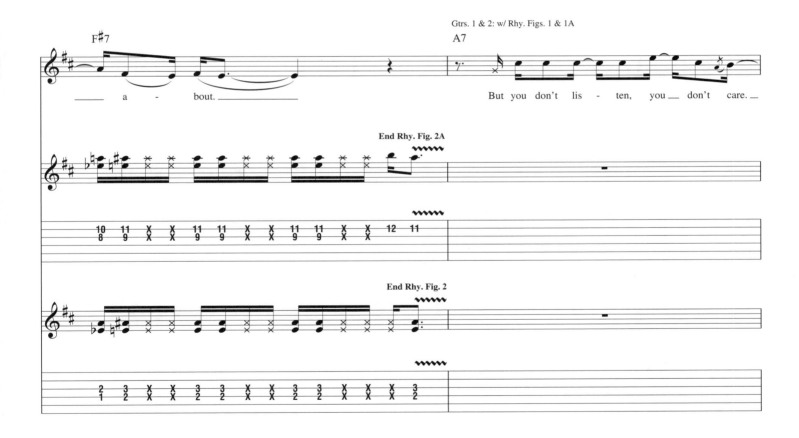

___ a - bout. ___ But you don't lis - ten, you ___ don't care. ___

___ No one tells ___ you what ___ to do ___ a - round ___ here, ___ uh. Well,

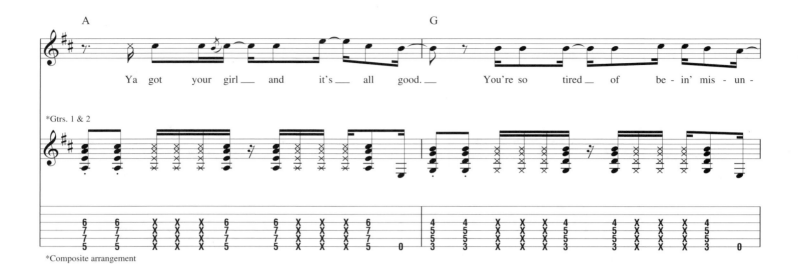

Ya got your girl ___ and it's ___ all good. ___ You're so tired ___ of be - in' mis - un-

*Gtrs. 1 & 2

*Composite arrangement

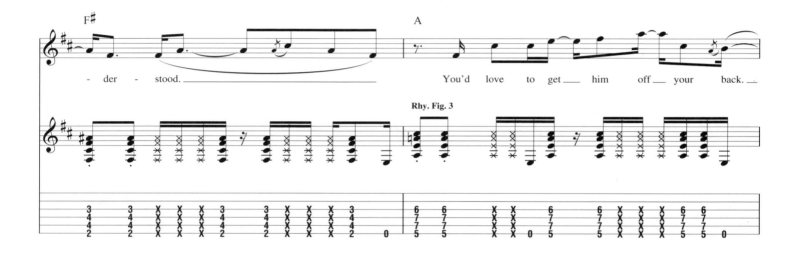

- der - stood. _____ You'd love to get ___ him off ___ your back. ___

Rhy. Fig. 3

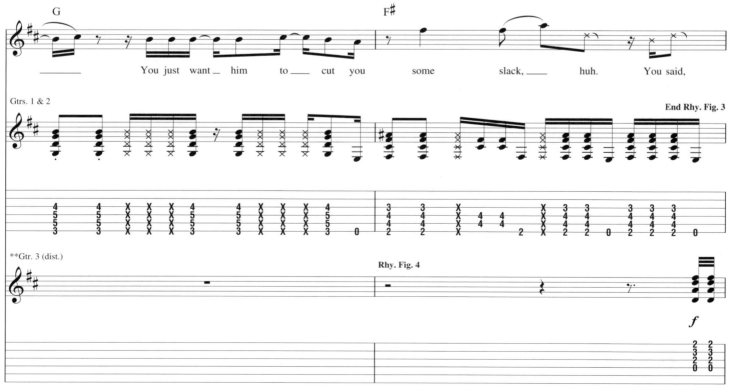

_____ You just want ___ him to ___ cut you some slack, ___ huh. You said,

Gtrs. 1 & 2

End Rhy. Fig. 3

**Gtr. 3 (dist.)

Rhy. Fig. 4

**Doubled throughout

Chorus

Gtr. 3 tacet

"He don't know — where I'm at." Yeah, — you get what you give, — don't you know, don't you know? — You get what

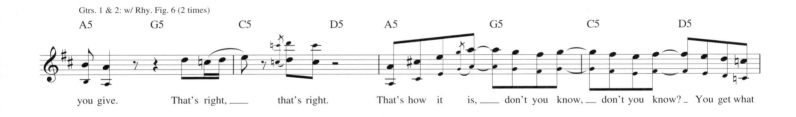

you give. That's right, —— that's right. That's how it is, — don't you know, — don't you know? — You get what

Verse

Gtr. 3 tacet

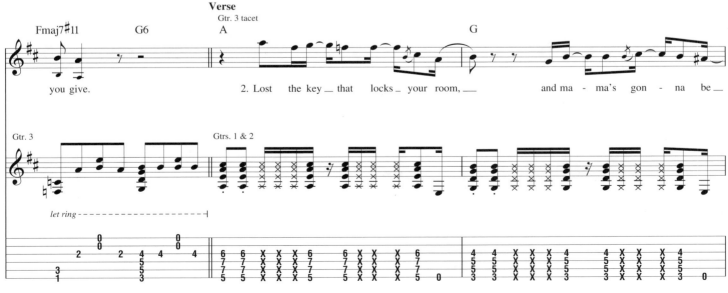

you give. 2. Lost the key — that locks — your room, —— and ma - ma's gon - na be —

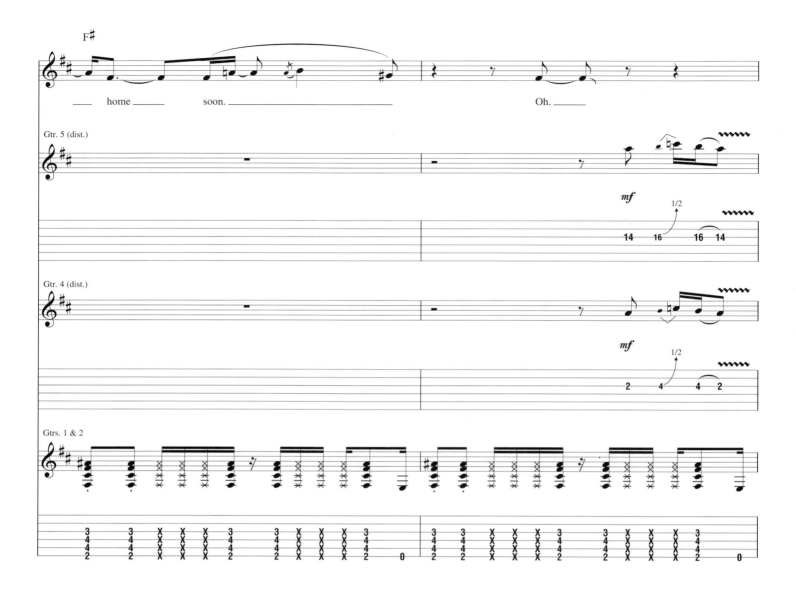

F#

home _____ soon. _____ Oh. _____

Gtr. 5 (dist.)

mf

Gtr. 4 (dist.)

mf

Gtrs. 1 & 2

Gtrs. 1 & 2: w/ Rhy. Fig. 3

A   G   F#

I guess this means __ you've got __ to __ lie. ___ You ain't got __ no oth - er al - i - bi. _____

Gtr. 5

Gtr. 4

Chorus

Gtrs. 1 & 2: w/ Rhy. Fig. 6 (3 times)
Gtr. 4 tacet

Gtr. 5: w/ Riff A (2 times)

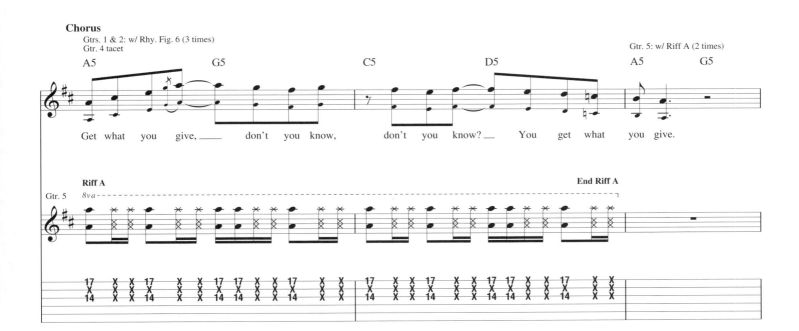

Get what you give, _____ don't you know, don't you know? You get what you give.

Riff A   End Riff A

Gtr. 5

Yeah. _____ Well, _____ that's how it is, _____ don't you know, _____ don't you know?_ You get what

Gtr. 4

Bridge

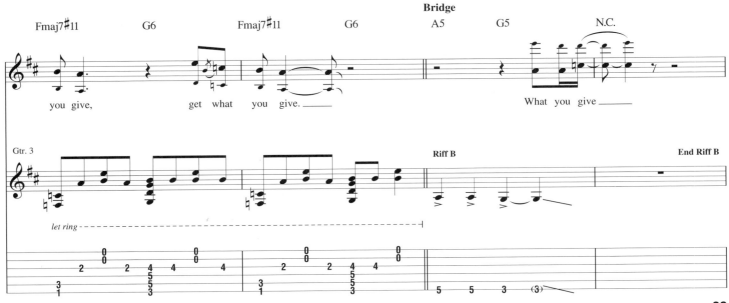

you give,   get what you give. _____   What you give _____

Gtr. 3   Riff B   End Riff B

let ring

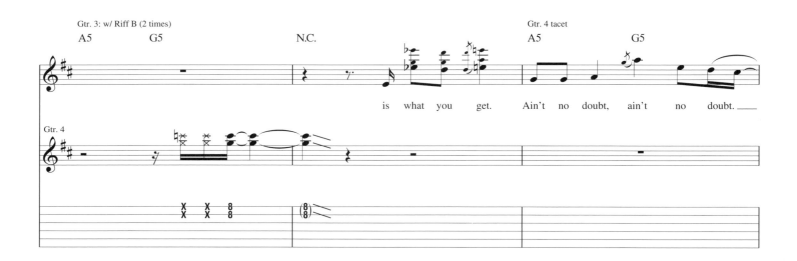

is what you get. Ain't no doubt, ain't no doubt.___

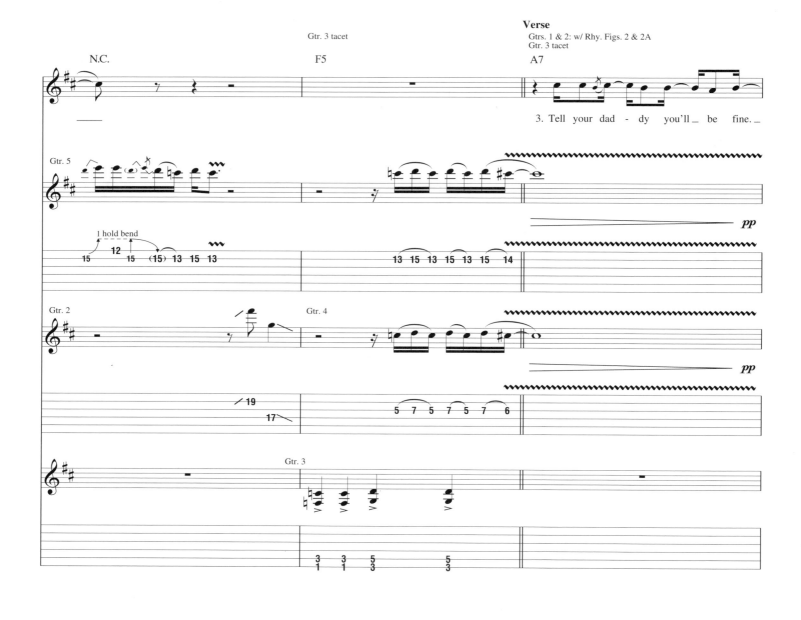

3. Tell your dad - dy you'll_ be fine._

___ Not to wor - ry, you'll_ get by._ Grow your hair_ and change_ your name._

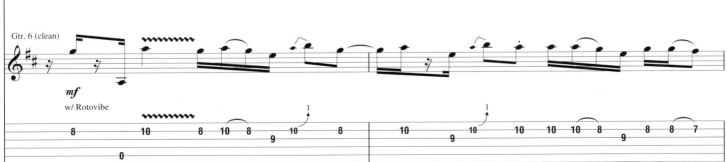

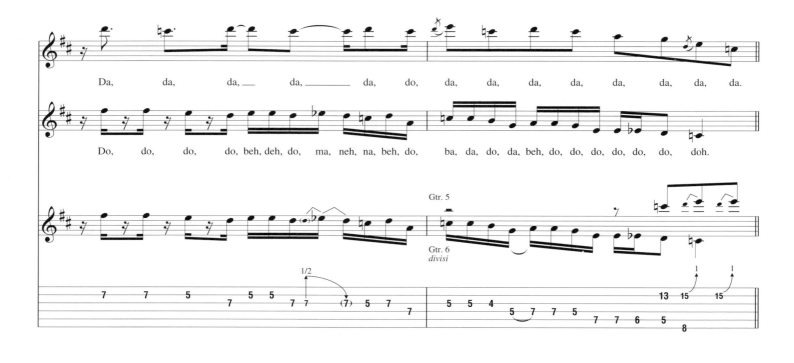

Da, da, da, ___ da, ___ da, do, da, da, da, da, da, da, da, da.

Do, do, do, do, beh, deh, do, ma, neh, na, beh, do, ba, da, do, da, beh, do, do, do, do, do, do, doh.

Outro-Chorus

Gtrs. 1, 2 & 3: w/ Rhy. Fig. 6 (3 times)
Gtr. 5: w/ Riff A (3 times)
Gtr. 6 tacet

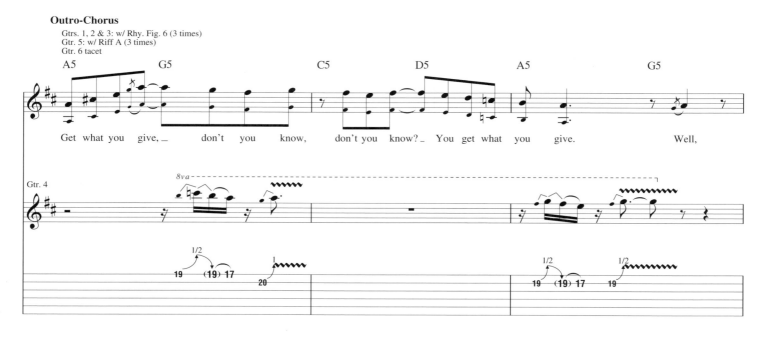

Get what you give, ___ don't you know, don't you know? ___ You get what you give. ___ Well,

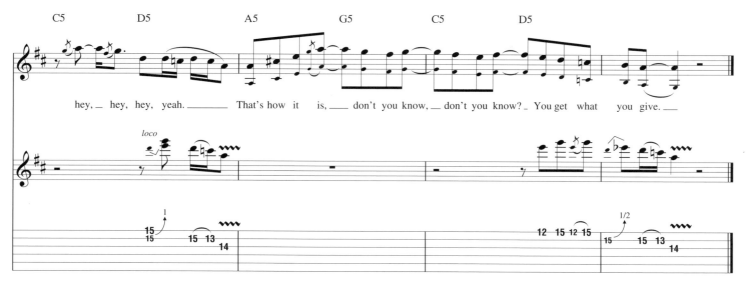

hey, ___ hey, hey, yeah. ___ That's how it is, ___ don't you know, don't you know? ___ You get what you give. ___

The One I Got

Words and Music by Jonny Lang and Marti Frederiksen

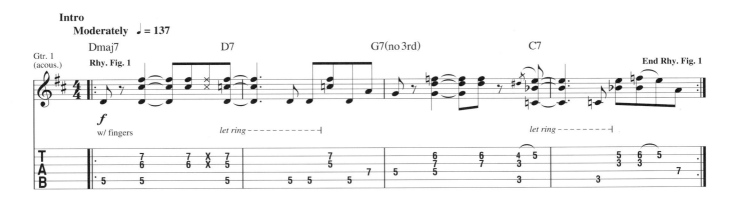

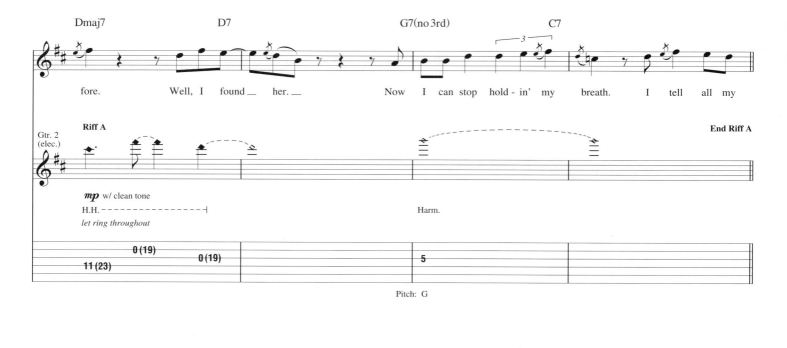

Dmaj7   D7   G7(no 3rd)   C7

fore.   Well, I   found _ her. _   Now   I   can   stop   hold - in'   my   breath.   I   tell   all   my

Pre-Chorus

E7   G7

friends _____   o - ver   and   o - ver _ a - gain. ___   I   said there

Chorus

ain't no wom-an like the one I've got, __ yes I know, __ yes I know. __ I said there

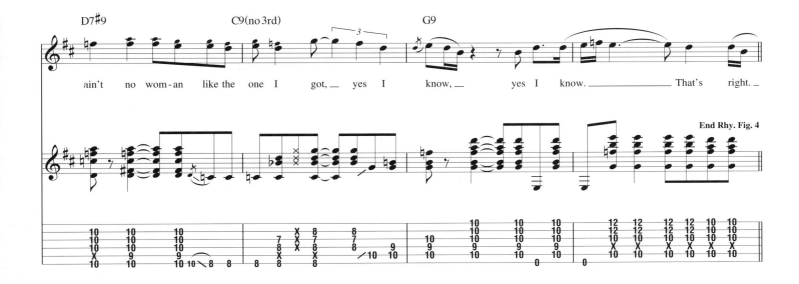

ain't no wom-an like the one I got, __ yes I know, __ yes I know. __ That's right. __

Interlude

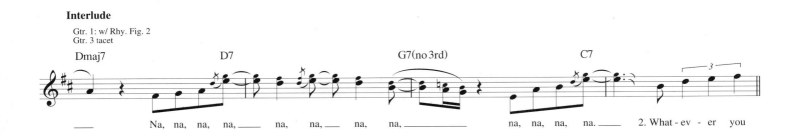

__ Na, na, na, na, __ na, na, __ na, na, __ na, na, na, na. 2. What-ev-er you

Verse

need, __ just tell __ me __ and I'll do all I can to please __ you. Yes, I don't

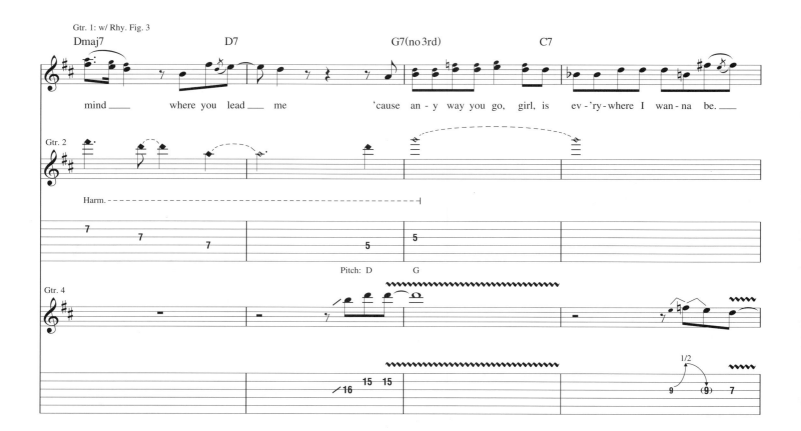

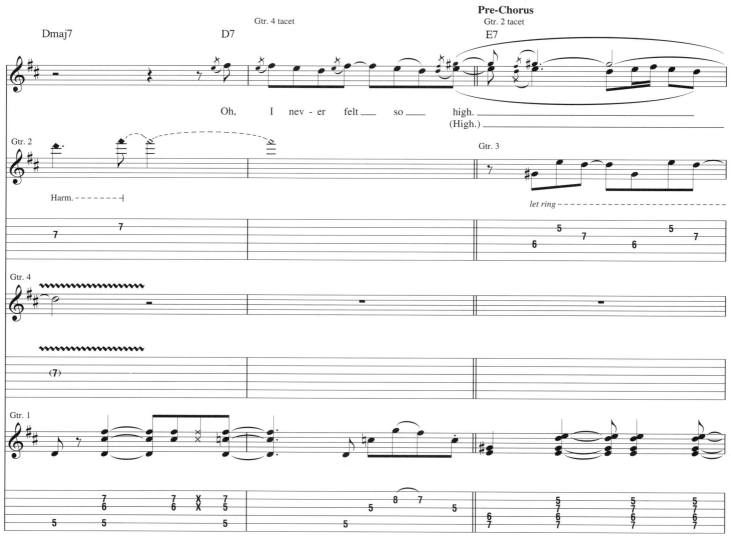

Bridge

Gtr. 4 tacet

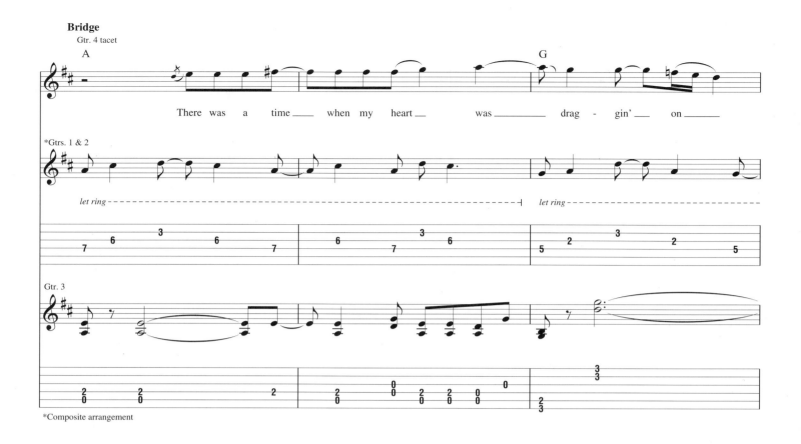

There was a time___ when my heart___ was___ drag - gin' ___ on ___

*Gtrs. 1 & 2

*Composite arrangement

the floor. ___

And I thank God___ for the day___ that I saw___

Pre-Chorus

friends ___ 'cause I ain't got time ___ left for them. ___ Be-cause there

Gtrs.
3 & 4

Gtr. 1

Chorus

Gtrs. 1 & 3: w/ Rhy. Fig. 4 (1 1/4 times)

ain't no wom-an like the one I've got, ___ yes I know, ___ yes I know. ___ Be-cause there

Gtr. 4

ain't — no feel-in' like the one I've got, — yes I know. _____ Oh yes, I

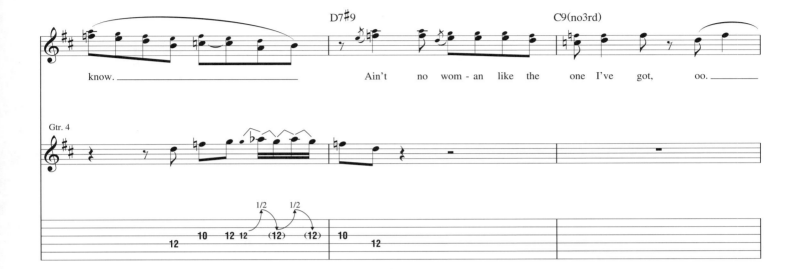

know. _____ Ain't no wom-an like the one I've got, oo. _____

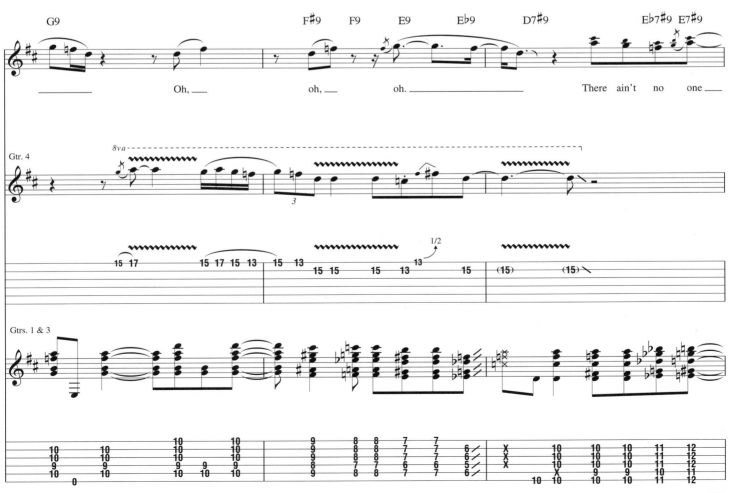

_____ Oh, — oh, — oh. _____ There ain't no one _____

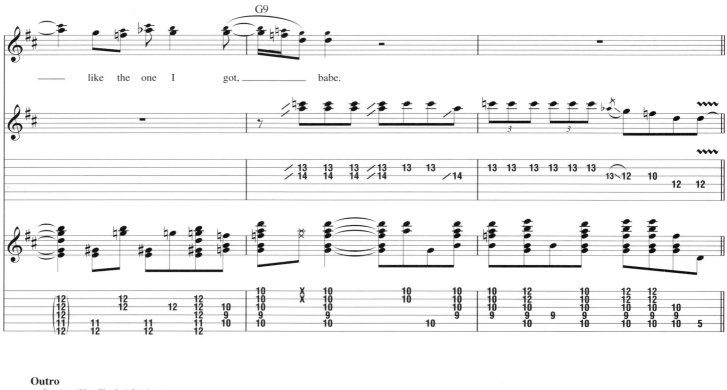

like the one I got, _____ babe.

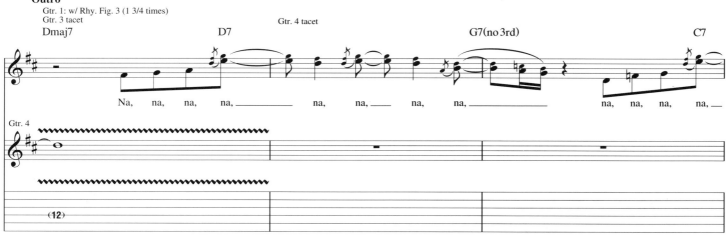

Outro

Gtr. 1: w/ Rhy. Fig. 3 (1 3/4 times)
Gtr. 3 tacet

Gtr. 4 tacet

Dmaj7   D7   G7(no 3rd)   C7

Na, na, na, na, _____ na, na, _____ na, na, _____ na, na, na, na, _____

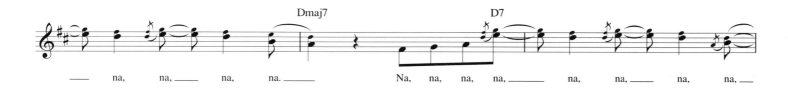

_____ na, na, _____ na, na.   Dmaj7   D7

Na, na, na, na, _____ na, na, _____ na, na, _____

G7(no 3rd)   C7   Dmaj7

na, na, na, na, _____ na, na, _____ na, na.

Touch

Words and Music by Jonny Lang and Marti Frederiksen

Chorus

'Cause I came a - live with your ___ touch. Your touch, it al - ways ___ sets me free. ___ I can't ___ get quite e -

*Piano arr. for gtr.

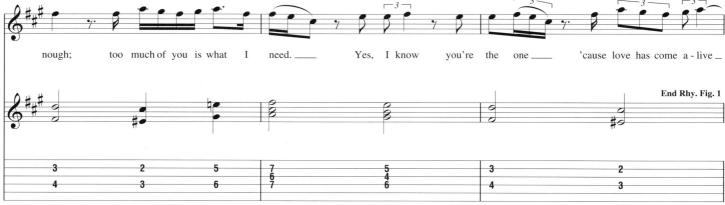

nough; too much of you is what I need. ___ Yes, I know you're the one ___ 'cause love has come a - live ___

Verse

Gtr. 3 tacet

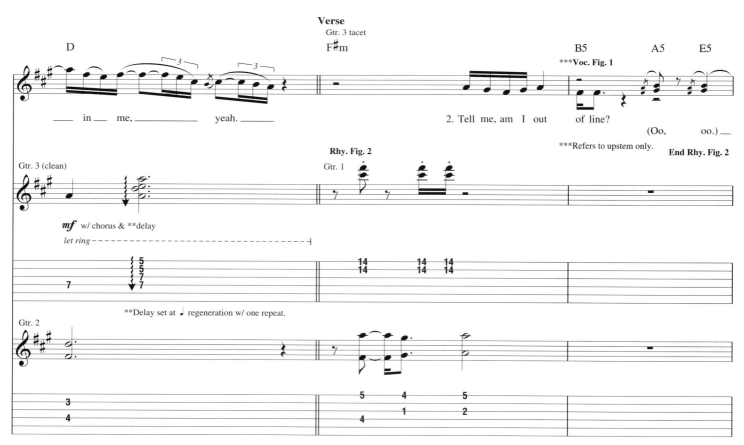

___ in ___ me, ___ yeah. ___ 2. Tell me, am I out of line?

(Oo, oo.)

***Refers to upstem only.

**Delay set at regeneration w/ one repeat.

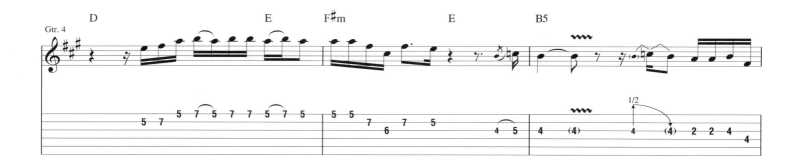

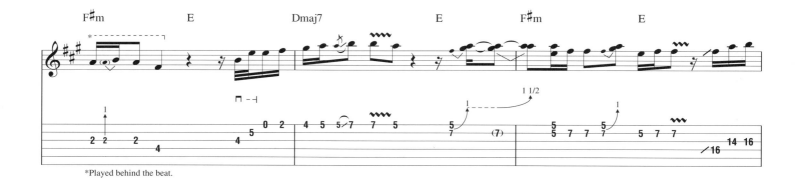

*Played behind the beat.

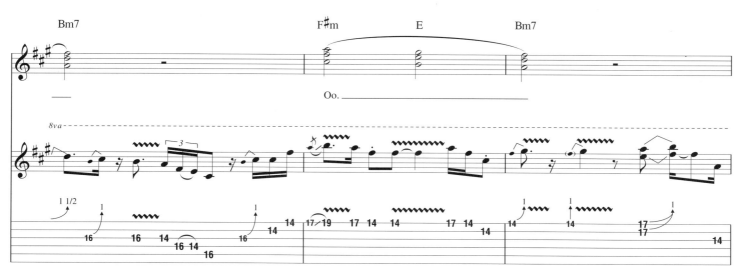

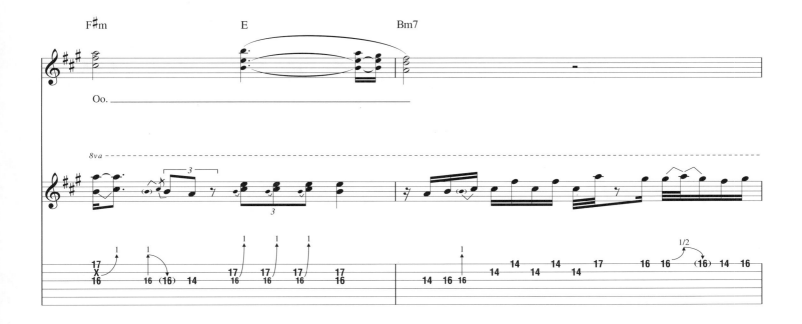

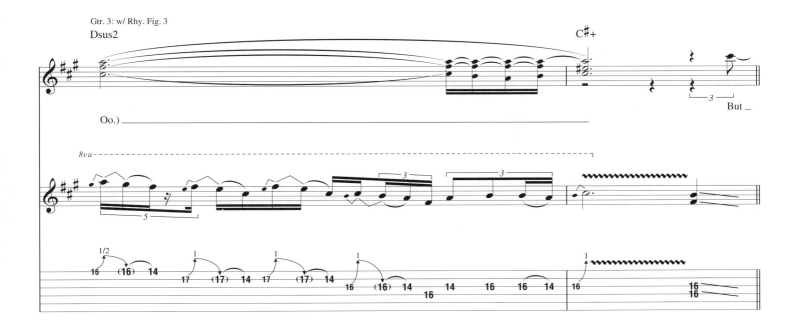

Verse

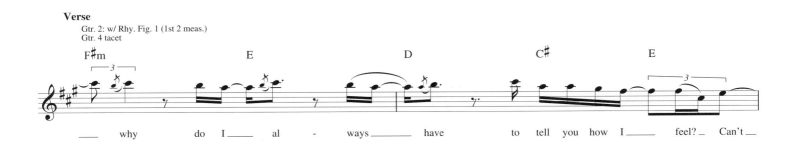

why do I al - ways have to tell you how I feel? Can't

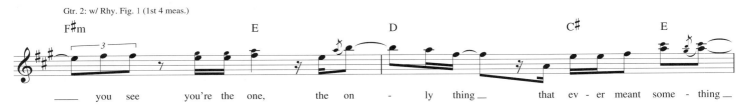

you see you're the one, the on - ly thing that ev - er meant some - thing

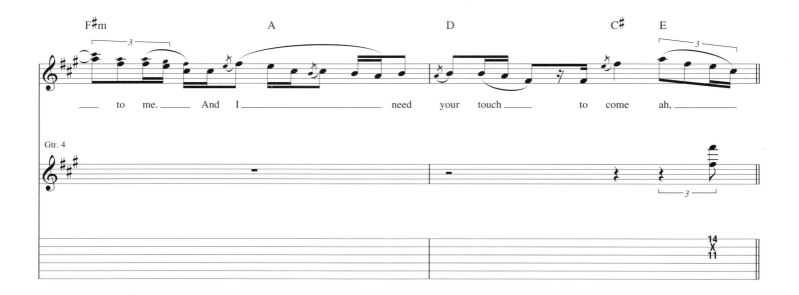

Outro-Guitar Solo

Bkgd. Voc.: w/ Voc. Fig. 1 (6 times)
Gtr. 2: w/ Rhy. Fig. 1 (1st 2 meas., 6 times)

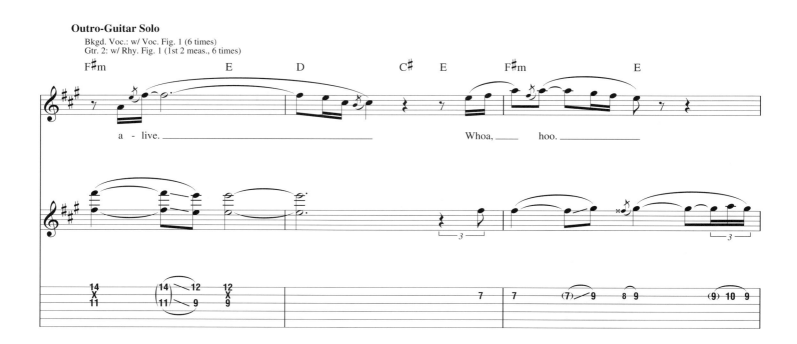

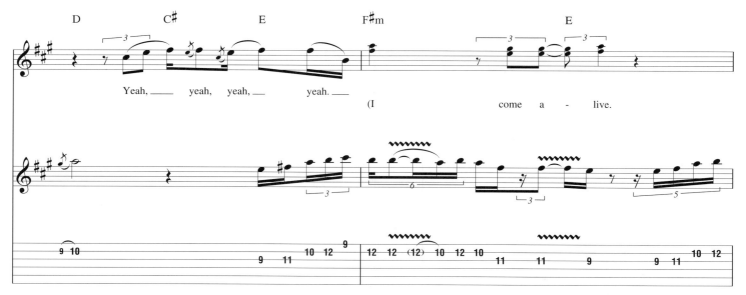

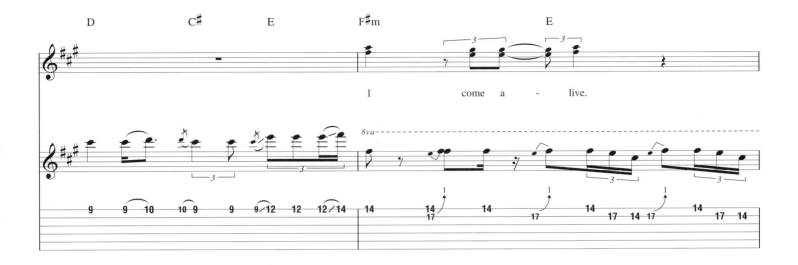

I come a - live.

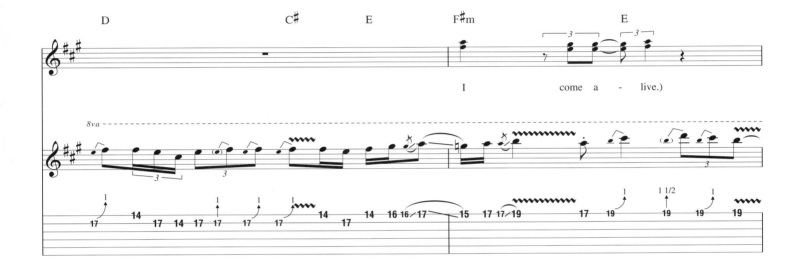

I come a - live.)

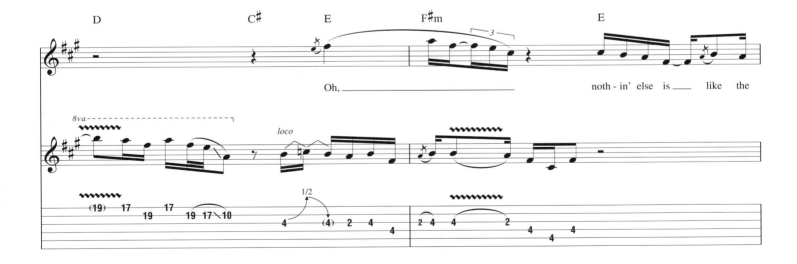

Oh, _____ noth - in' else is ___ like the

Gtr. 4 tacet

way you make ___ me come ___ a - live, _____ babe.

Beautiful One

Words and Music by Jonny Lang and Marti Frederiksen

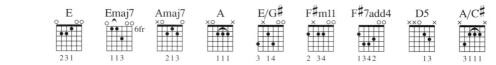

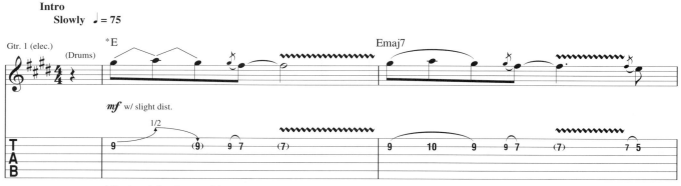

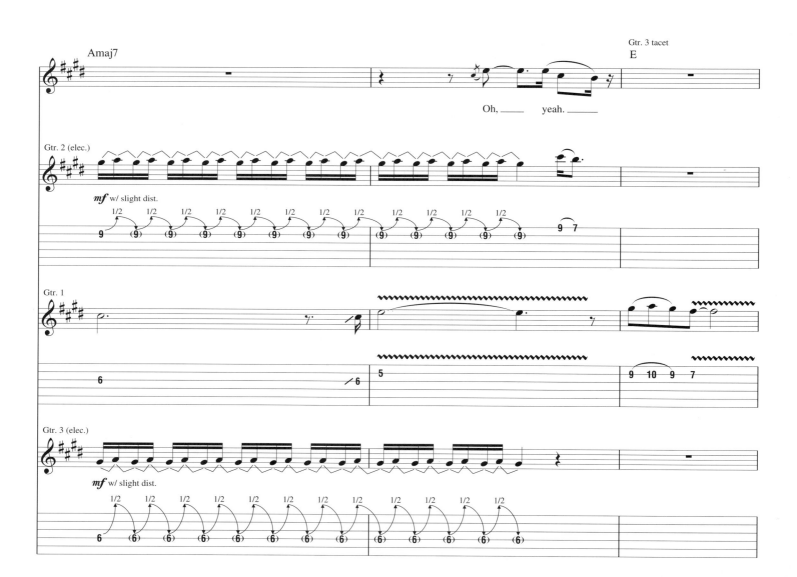

*Chord symbols reflect overall harmony.

Some- how _ in my mind, al - ways knew _ I'd find _____ my

let ring throughout

Gtr. 4

Gtr. 5 (elec.)

mp w/ slight dist.

let ring throughout

Chorus

Gtr. 4 tacet

Rhy. Fig. 1

Gtrs. 6 & 7
(acous.)

mp

let ring throughout

beau - ti - ful one, ___ beau - ti - ful child, _ my ev - 'ry - thing. _

Gtr. 2

Riff B

mf

Gtr. 3

Riff B1

Gtr. 5 **Riff A**

2. So much _ you give, _ so much to live ____ for, _ and I wan - na give _

____ it all back ____ to you. And if it means _ pour - ing my heart ____ out _____

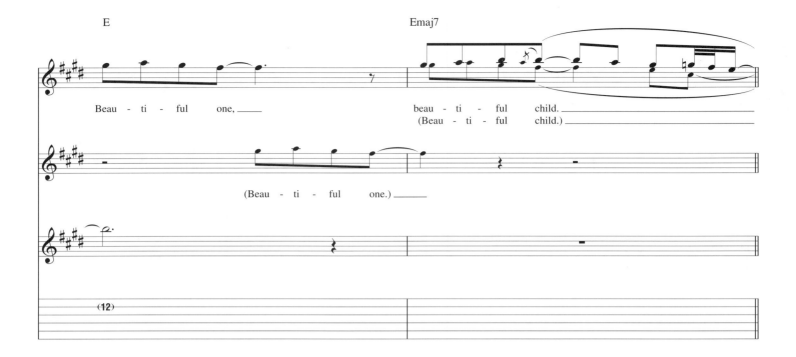

Bridge

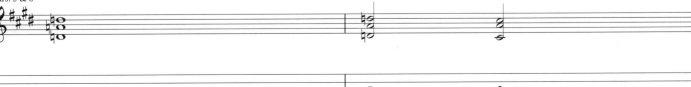

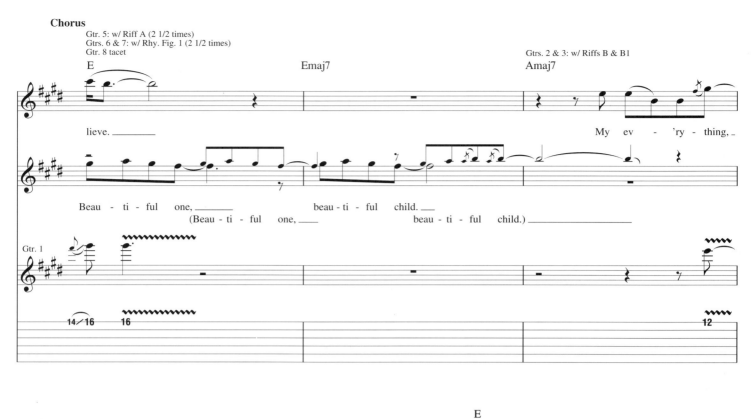

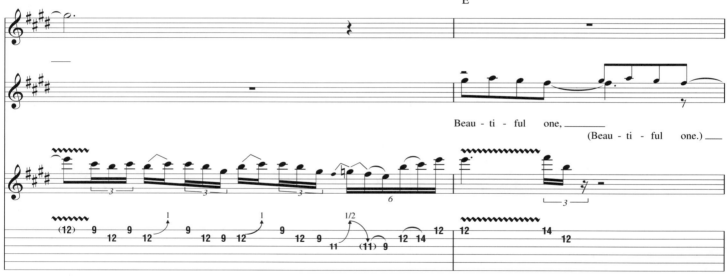

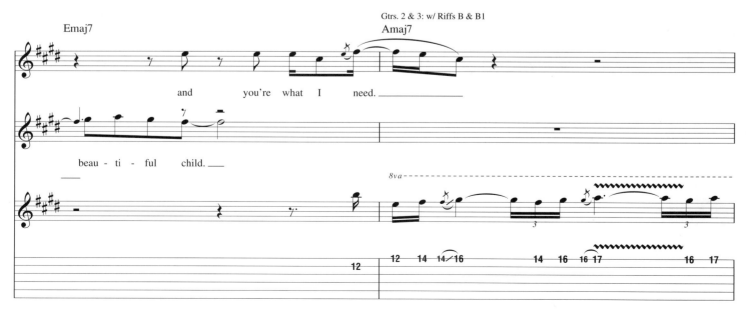

If We Try

Words and Music by Jonny Lang and Marti Frederiksen

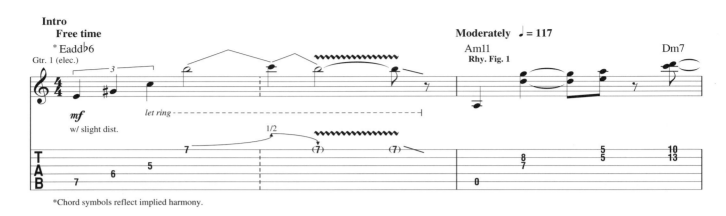

*Chord symbols reflect implied harmony.

1. We walked a - way be - fore we said good - bye.___ That ain't right,___ ba - by.   No.___

I al - ways thought we'd stand the test of time.___ I was wrong,___ ba - by.   Well.___

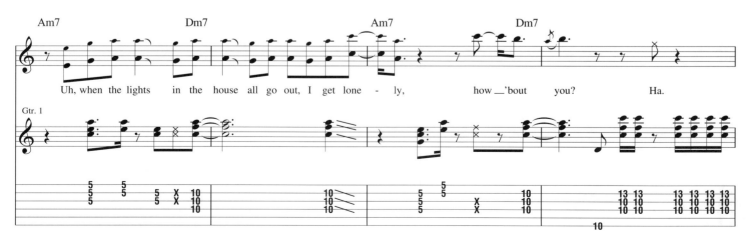

Uh, when the lights   in the house all go out, I get lone - ly,   how __'bout   you?   Ha.

Chorus

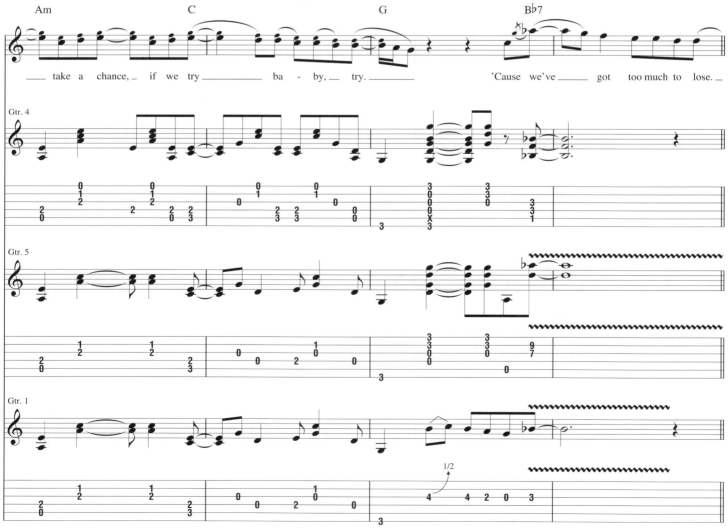

Interlude

Gtrs. 4 & 5 tacet

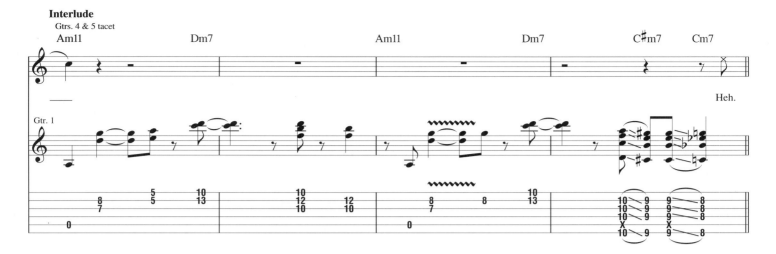

Heh.

Gtr. 1

Verse

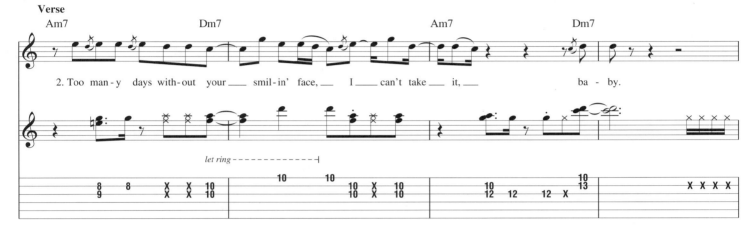

2. Too man-y days with-out your ___ smil-in' face, ___ I ___ can't take ___ it, ___ ba - by.

let ring ----------------|

Gtr. 2: w/ Rhy. Fig. 2
Gtr. 3: w/ Riff A

I ___ pre-tend that I'm feel-in' fine, ___ but I'm fak - in'. ___ Words ___ just ___ can't de - scribe, ___

Pre-Chorus

Gtr. 1: tacet
Gtr. 3: w/ Riff B

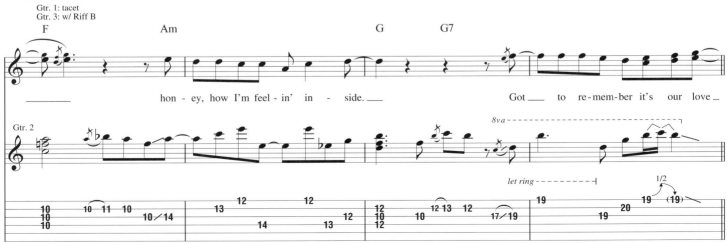

___ hon - ey, how I'm feel - in' in - side. ___ Got ___ to re-mem-ber it's our love ___

Gtr. 2

8va --------------------------------|

let ring ---------|

1/2

Chorus
Gtr. 2 tacet
Gtr. 4: w/ Rhy. Fig. 3

____ on the line. ___ We should try, _____ ba - by, ___ try. ___ I know we can make it if we both ___

___ take a chance, ___ if we try ____ ba - by, ___ try. ____ 'Cause we've ___ got ___ so much ___ to lose. ___

Bridge

Gtrs. 1, 4 & 5 tacet

Ev-'ry day that goes ___ by, I wish I ___ could some-how get you to un-der - stand.

I fig-ure if you re-mem-ber how good we were to-geth-er, that you'll wan -

Guitar Solo

Gtr. 6 tacet

na be with me a - gain. ___

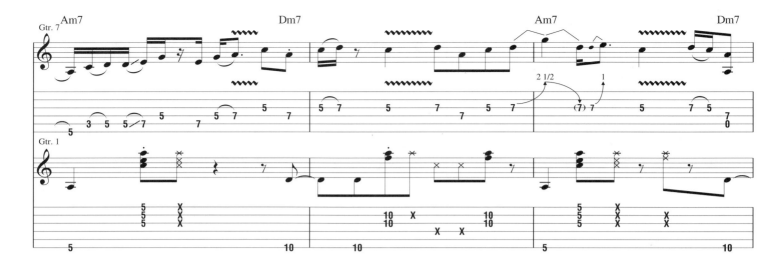

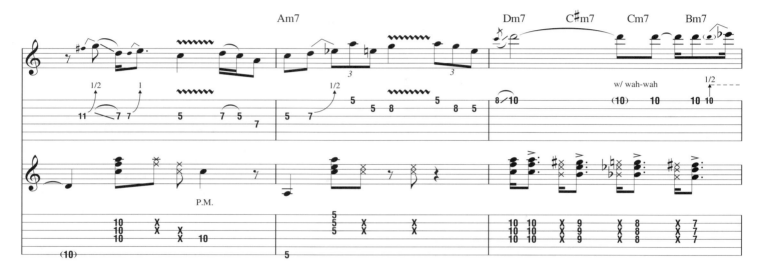

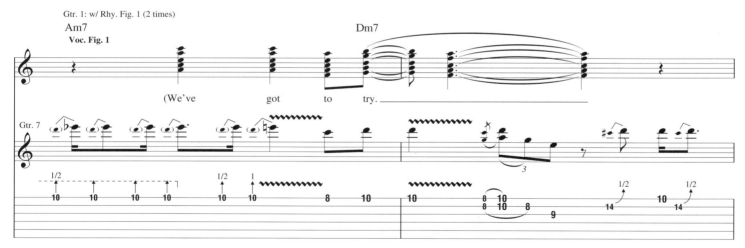

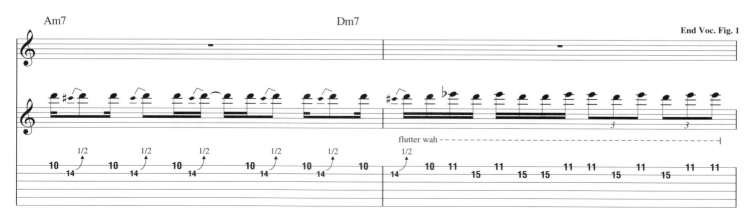

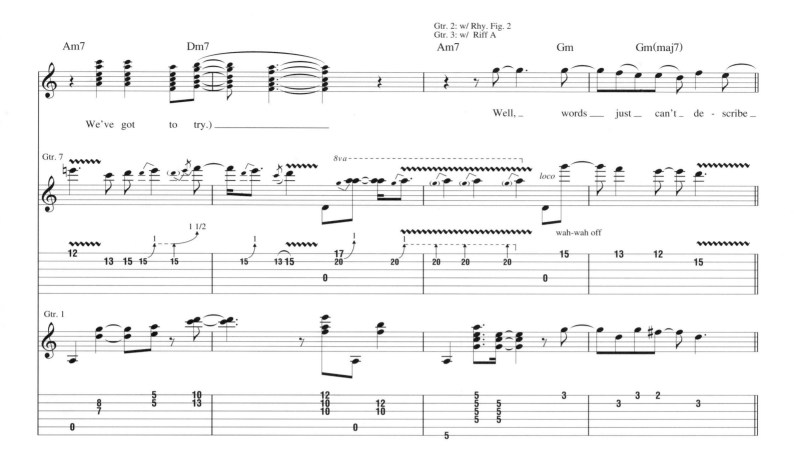

Pre-Chorus

Chorus
Gtr. 1: w/ Riff C
Gtr. 4: w/ Rhy. Fig. 3
Gtr. 5: w/ Rhy. Fig. 4

Ba - by, don't for - get ___ that it's our love ___ on the line, ___

Na, na, na, ___ na, na, na, ___ na, na, na, ___

___ so ___ we should ___ try. ___

Oh, we got to get back to where

___ na, ___ na, ___ na.) ___

Outro

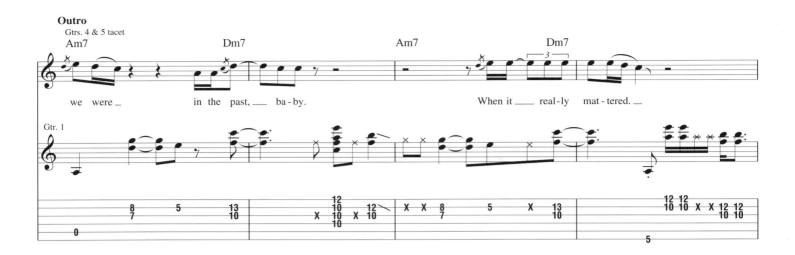

we were __ in the past, __ ba - by. When it __ real - ly mat - tered. __

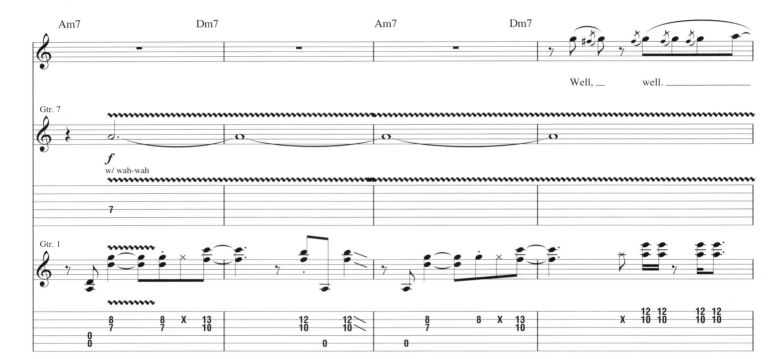

Well, __ well. ____

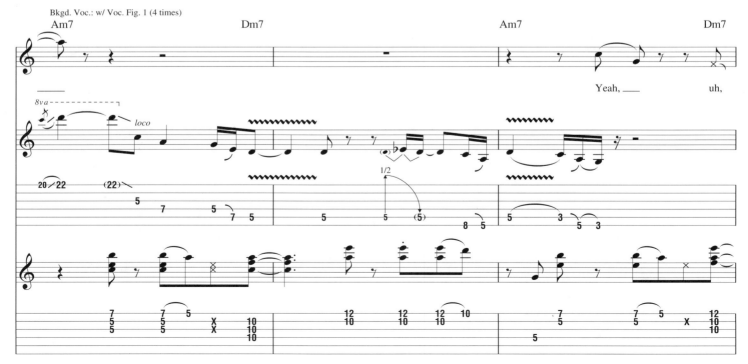

Yeah, __ uh,

80

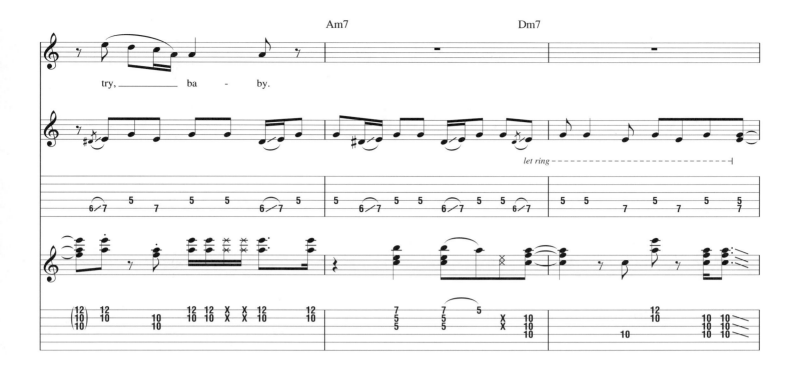

try, _____ ba - by.

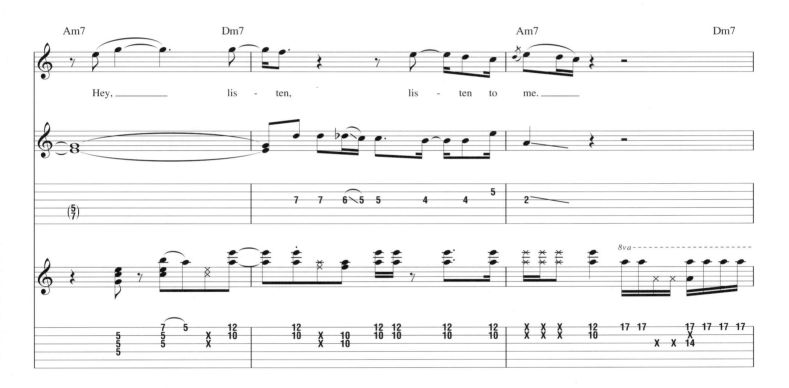

Hey, _____ lis - ten, _____ lis - ten to me. _____

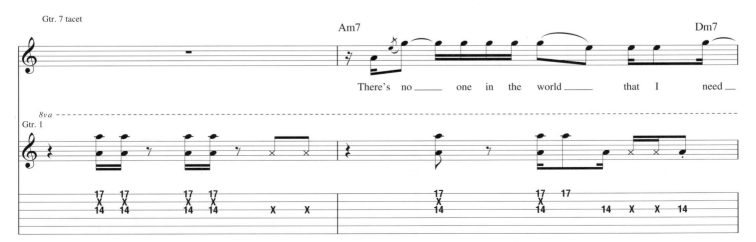

There's no _____ one in the world _____ that I need _____

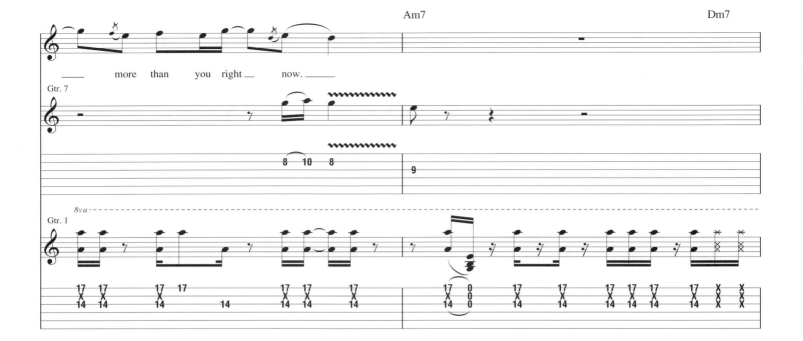

more than you right ___ now.

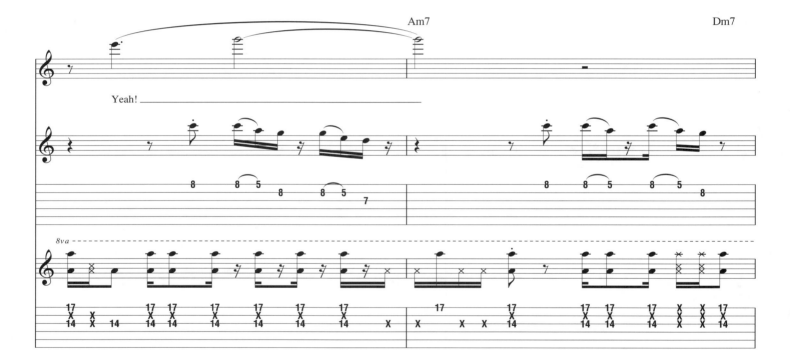

Yeah! ___

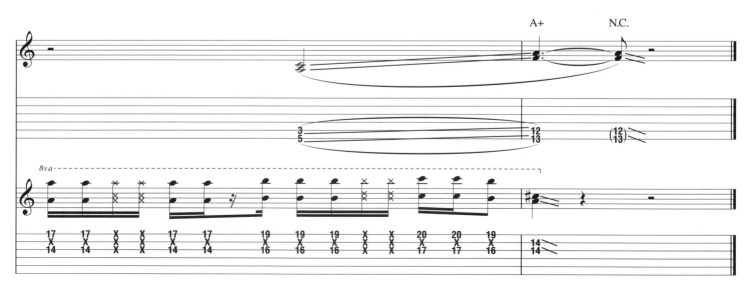

Goodbye Letter

Words and Music by Jonny Lang and Marti Frederiksen

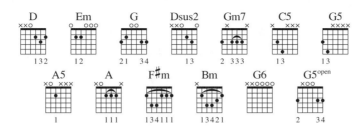

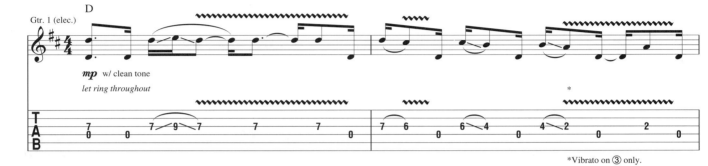

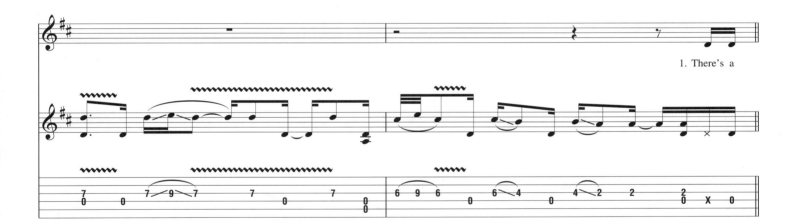

I don't have to read it 'cause I al-read-y know, _____ oh, _____ oh.

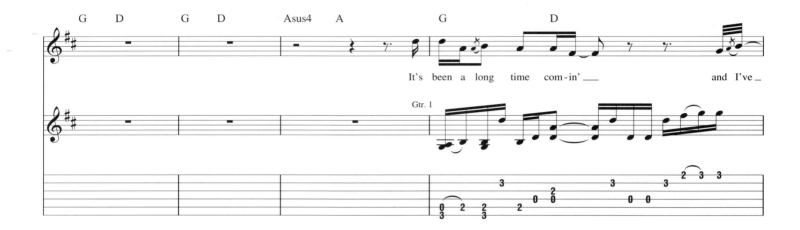

It's been a long time com-in' _____ and I've _

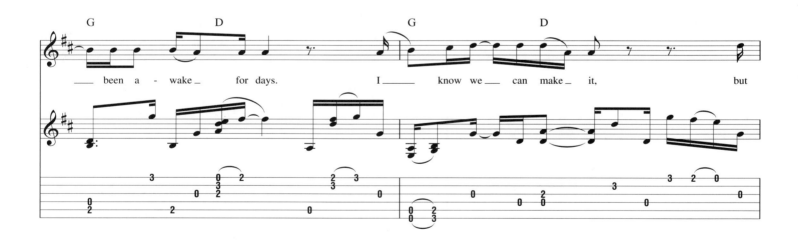

_____ been a - wake _ for days. I _____ know we _ can make _ it, but

things have got _ to change. _____ Your words say it's hope - less, _ but

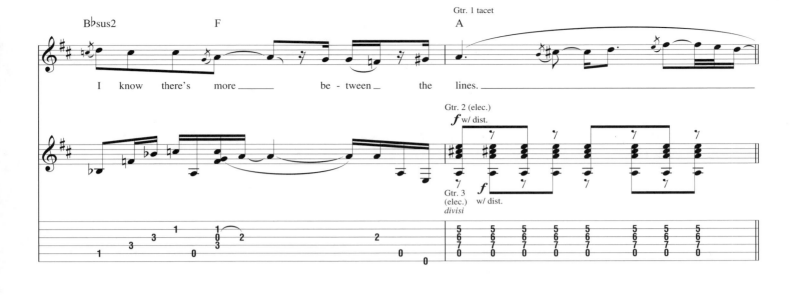

I know there's more _____ be - tween ____ the lines. _____

Chorus

____ Good - bye. _____ Is this how you want _____ it? _____

*Two gtrs. arr. for one.

**Composite arrangement

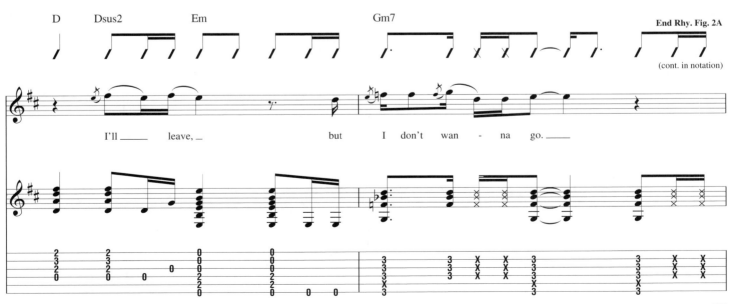

I'll _____ leave, ___ but I don't wan - na go. _____

And I'll wait, ___ but I can't wait for - ev - er ___ for you to say good -

Interlude

Gtr. 5 tacet

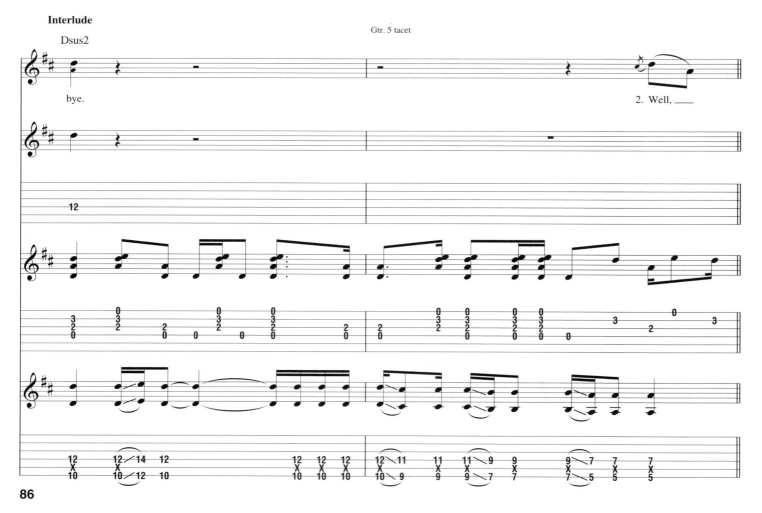

bye.

2. Well, ___

Verse

Gtr. 1: w/ Rhy. Fig. 1 (1 1/2 times)
Gtr. 2 tacet

may - be I'm just dream - in', but I know dreams __ come true and

I'm still here __ be - liev - ing that God made me __ for you. __ If

we could just start o - ver, get back where we ___ be - gan, ___ we're

bet - ter off to - geth - er. ___ It does - n't have to end, ___ oh. ___

Chorus

Gtrs. 1 & 6 tacet
Gtrs. 2, 3 & 4: w/ Rhy. Figs. 2 & 2A

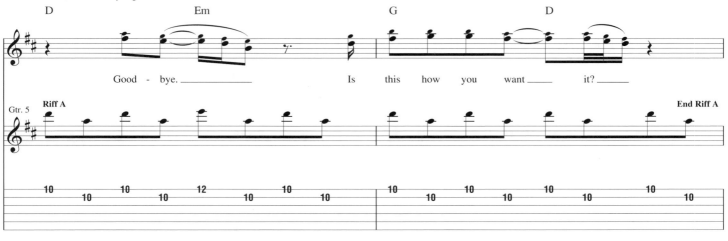

Good - bye. _____ Is this how you want _____ it? _____

Gtr. 5: w/ Riff A

I'll leave, _____ but I don't wan - na go. _____

And I'll wait, _____ but I won't wait for - ev - er _____ for you to say good -

Guitar Solo

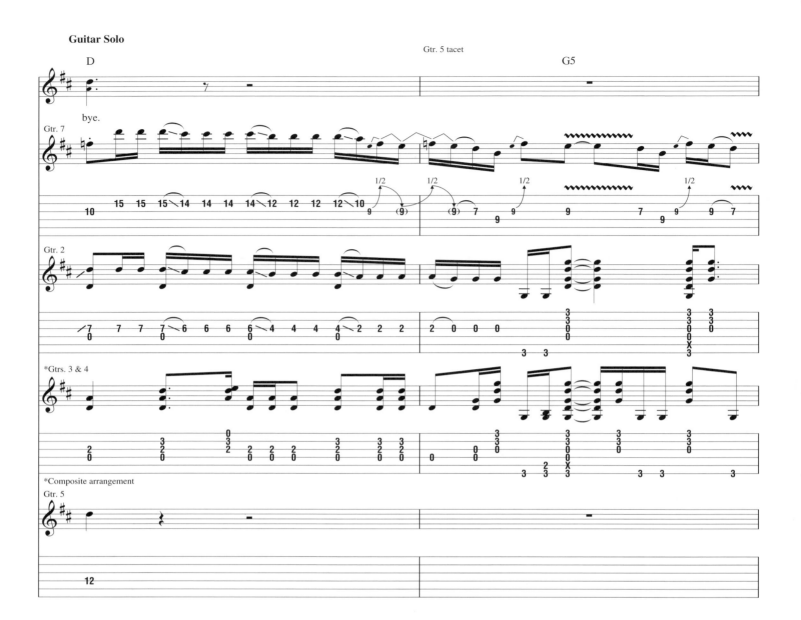

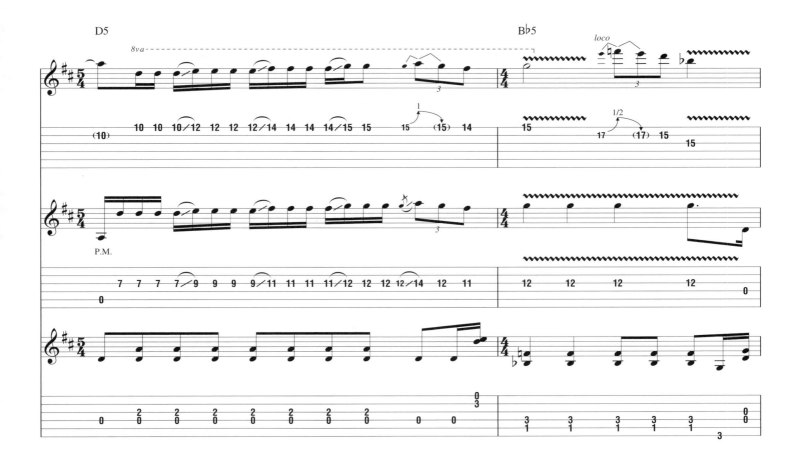

Chorus
Gtrs. 2 & 3: w/ Rhy. Fig. 2 (1st 4 meas.)
Gtr. 4: w/ Rhy. Fig. 2A
Gtr. 5: w/ Riff A (2 times)

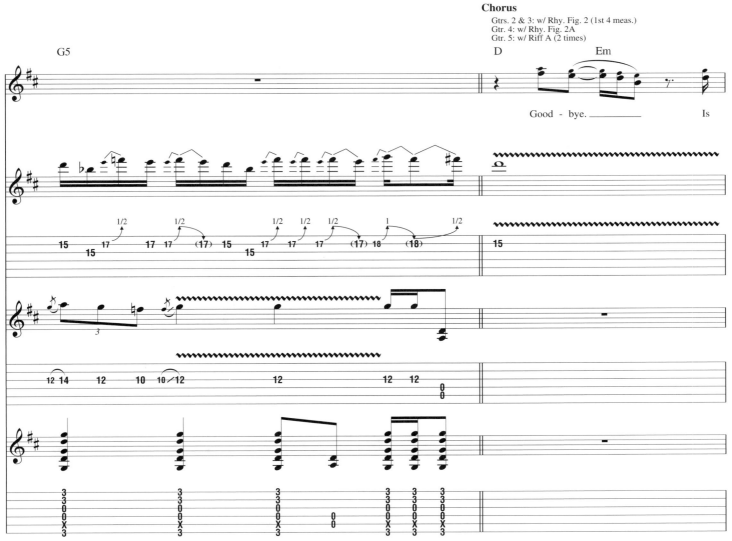

Good - bye. _____ Is

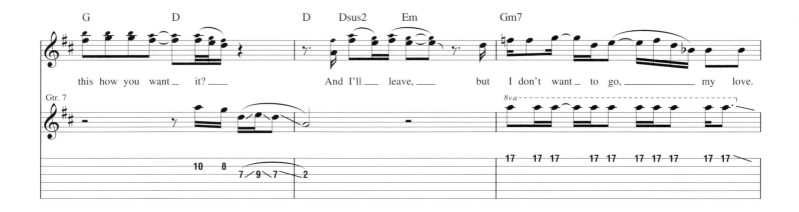

this how you want it? And I'll leave, but I don't want to go, my love.

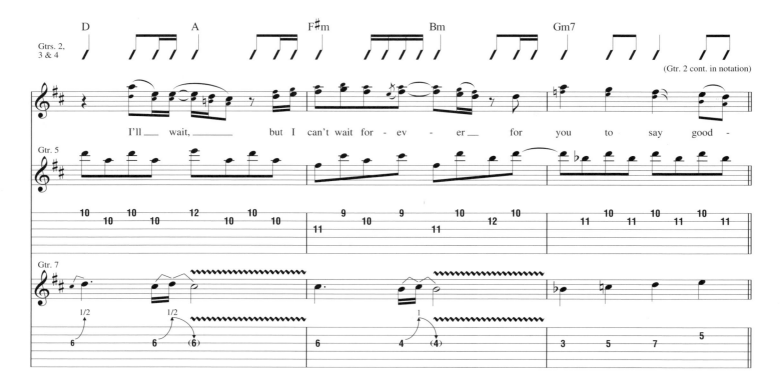

I'll wait, but I can't wait for-ev-er for you to say good-

Outro

bye, good-bye.

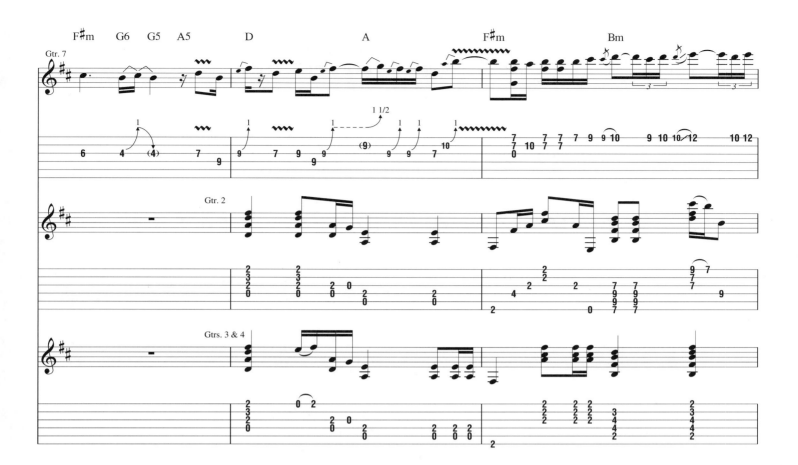

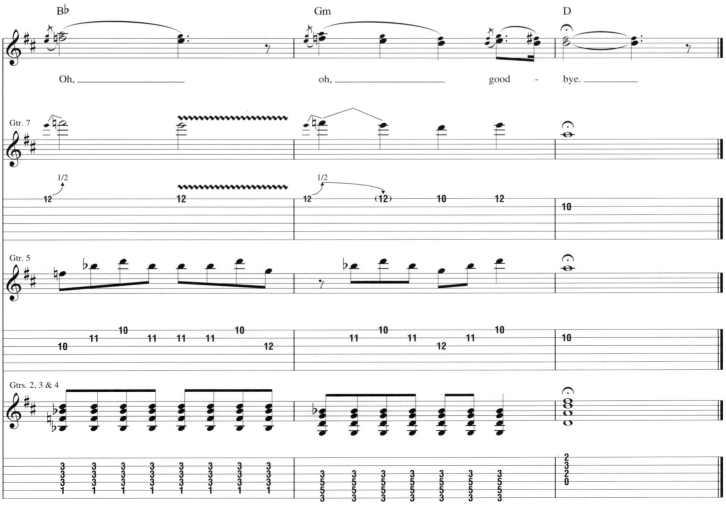

Save Yourself

Words and Music by Jonny Lang and Marti Frederiksen

*Chord symbols reflect implied harmony.

Nev-er a prob-lem _____ here on the out - side. _____ You're good at dis-guis - in' the

truth. _____

Af - ter you wake _ up _____ out of the night - mare, how do you cast _ out _ the

*Gtrs. 3 & 4

*Composite arrangement

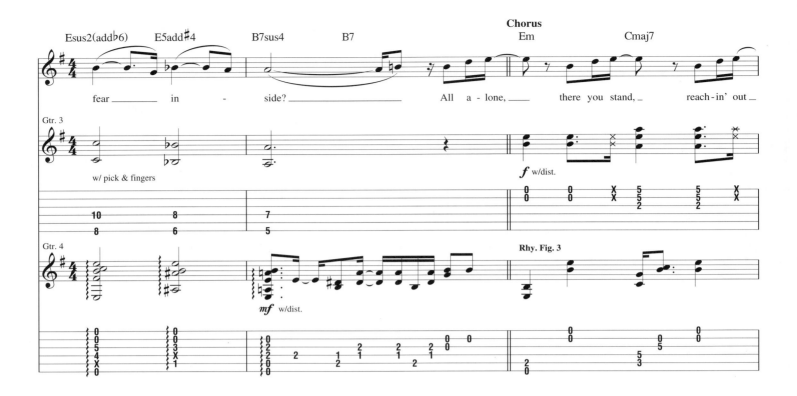

if you want ___ to save _ your-self. _____ Don't let the past haunt your mind, ___ you should leave ___

___ it all ___ be-hind. ___ Come with me _____ if you want ___ to save _ your-self. _____ There's

some-thin' in the way, ___ it's got-ten in-to you. ___ You've learned to love ___ and chains. _____ Through ___

Guitar Solo
Gtrs. 2 & 3: w/ Rhy. Figs. 1 & 2 (1 3/4 times)

___ the nee-dle's eye _____ can you es - cape? _____

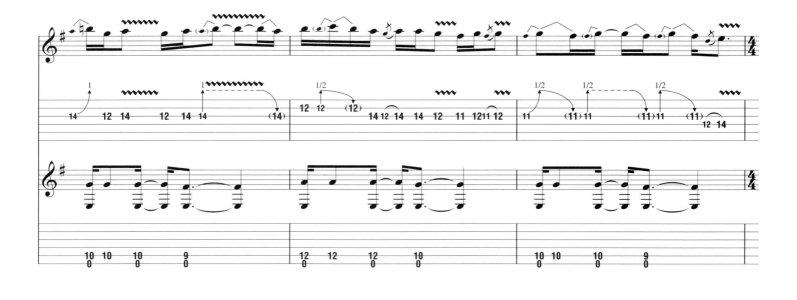

To Love Again

Words and Music by Jonny Lang and Marti Frederiksen

End Rhy. Fig. 1

(cont. in slashes)

un - der con - trol. _____   Yeah, ì was dy - in'. I _____   did-n't e - ven know. _____

Chorus

Rhy. Fig. 2

Gtr. 1

w/ pick

I _____ need - ed some - thin'.   You _____ showed me how to love a - gain, _____   to _____ love

Gtr. 3   **Riff A**
(elec.)

8va -

mf

w/ dist.

Gtr. 2
(elec.)   Rhy. Fig. 2A

f

w/ dist.

103

a - gain. _____ When __ I had noth - in', you __ showed me how to love

a - gain, __ how to love __ a, a - gain. _____

Interlude
Gtr. 2 tacet

Guitar Solo

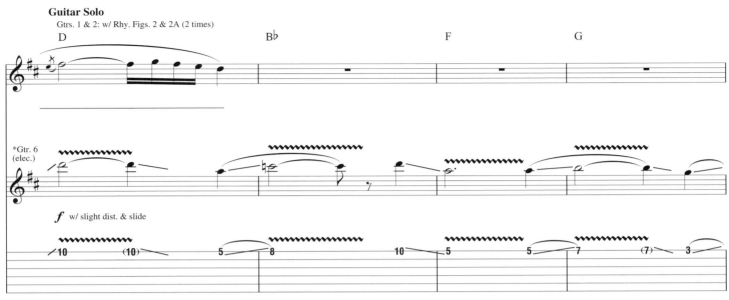

*Doubled throughout

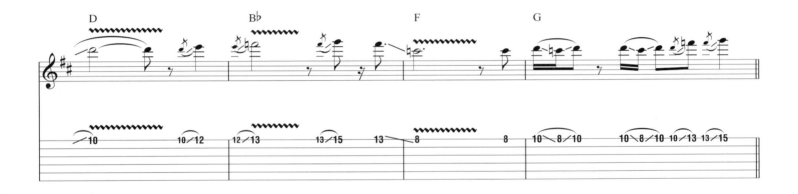

Chorus

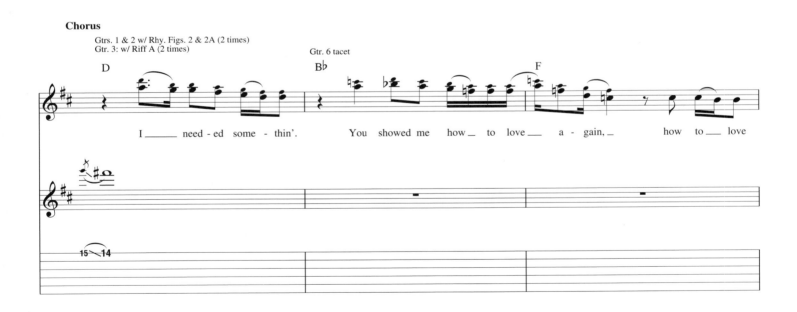

I _____ need-ed some-thin'.   You showed me how__ to love__ a - gain,__   how to __ love

a - gain.____   When __ I had noth - in',__   you __ showed me how to love __

Outro-Guitar Solo

Gtrs. 1 & 2: w/ Rhy. Figs. 2 & 2A (2 times)
Gtr. 3: w/ Riff A (2 times)

a - gain, _____ how to love a - gain.

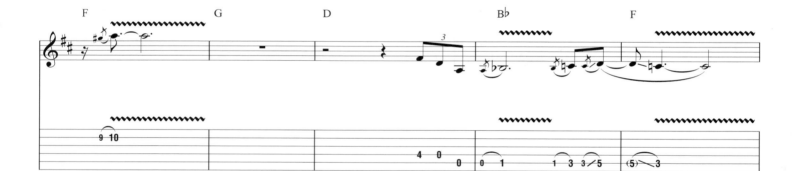

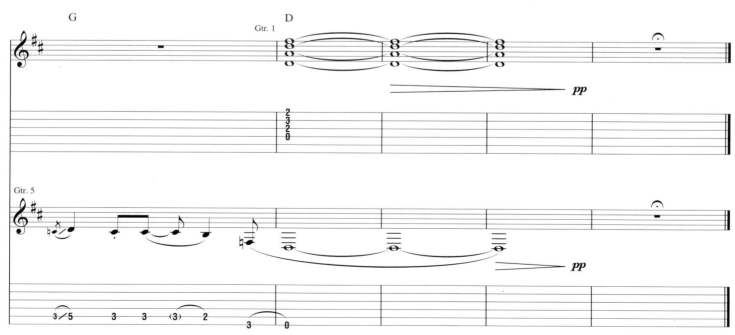

108

Happiness and Misery

Words and Music by Jonny Lang and Marti Frederiksen

Intro
Moderately ♩ = 144

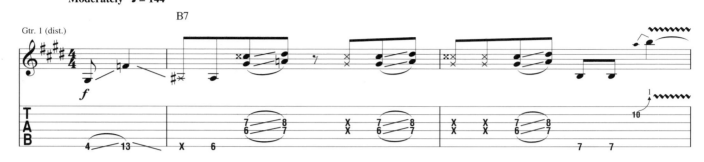

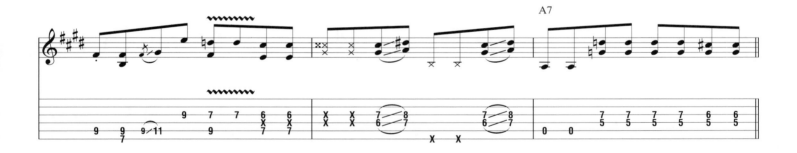

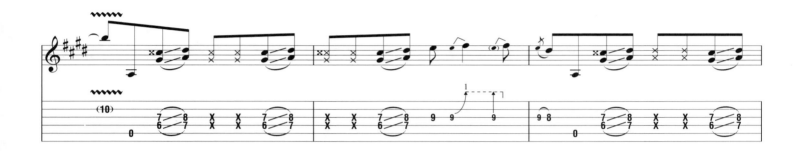

1. A thou - sand peo - ple here, _____ but I'm _____ a - lone.

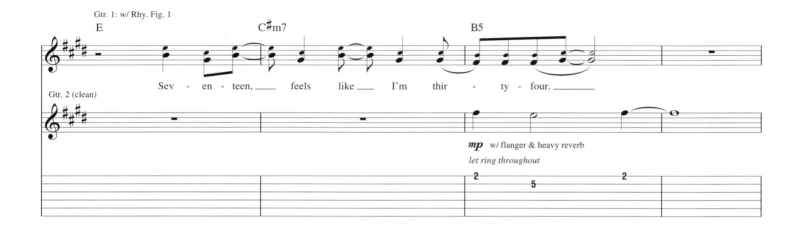

I need __ a cure. _____

Chorus
Gtrs. 2 & 3 tacet

E5   C5   G5   B5

Hap - pi - ness ____ and mis - er - y. ____ I'm up ____ and down, __ so ___ con - fused. _ I wan -

Gtr. 5
(dist.)   **Riff A**

*Gtrs. 1
& 4 (dist.)   **Rhy. Fig. 2**

*Composite arrangement

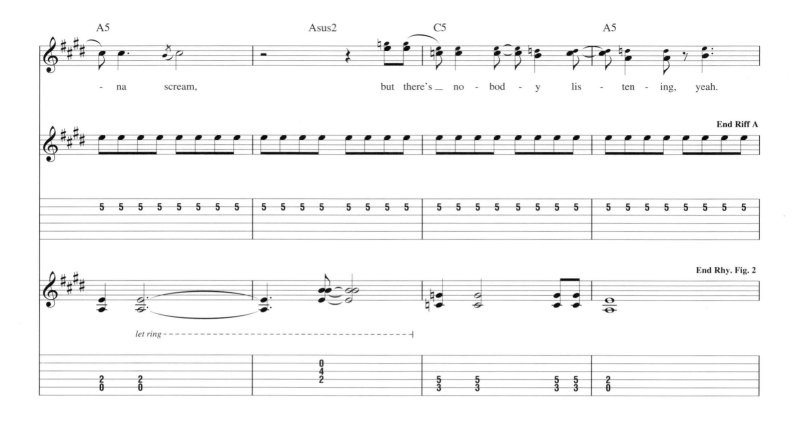

- na scream, but there's __ no - bod - y lis - ten - ing, yeah.

End Riff A

End Rhy. Fig. 2

let ring -

Gtrs. 1 & 4: w/ Rhy. Fig. 2 (1st 6 meas.)
Gtr. 5: w/ Riff A

Stop the war __ in - side __ of me. __ Pull __ the plug __ and kill __

__ the lights. __ I can't __ break free. __ It's hap -

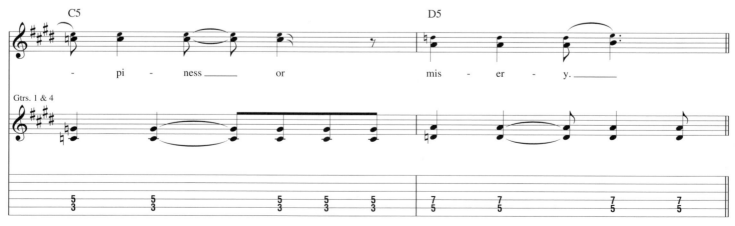

- pi - ness __ or mis - er - y. __

Gtrs. 1 & 4

Verse
Half-time feel

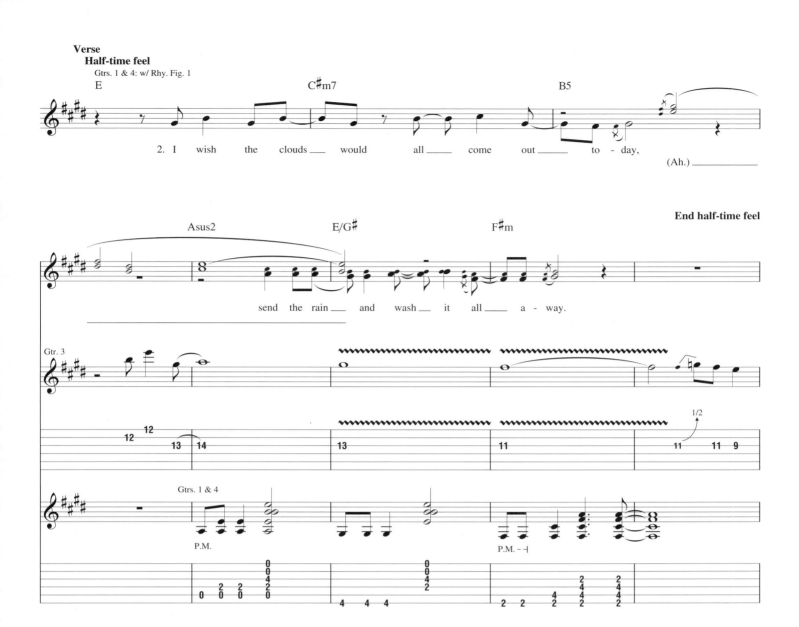

End half-time feel

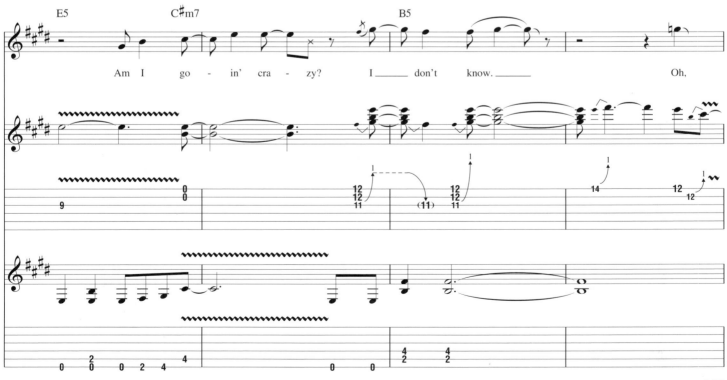

I won-der, will an-y-bod-y miss me if ___ I go? ___ Oh, ho, ___ ho, ho. ___

Chorus

Gtrs. 1 & 4: w/ Rhy. Fig. 2 (1 3/4 times)
Gtr. 5: w/ Riff A (2 times)

Hap-pi-ness ___ and mis-er-y. ___ I'm up ___ and down, ___ so ___ con-fused. ___ I wan-

Gtr. 3

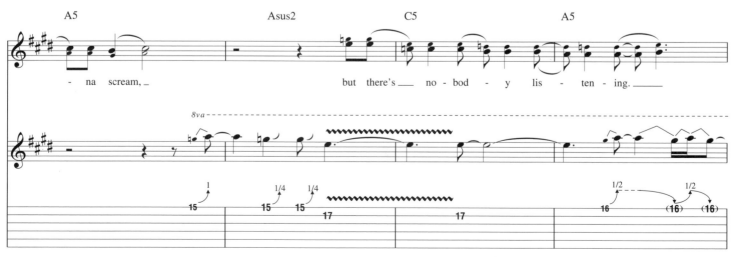

- na scream, ___ but there's ___ no-bod-y lis-ten-ing. ___

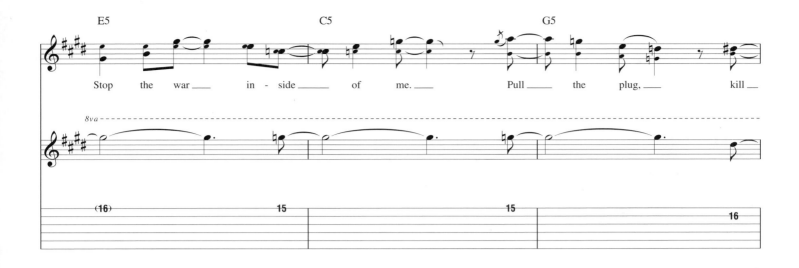

Stop the war ___ in - side ___ of me. ___ Pull ___ the plug, ___ kill

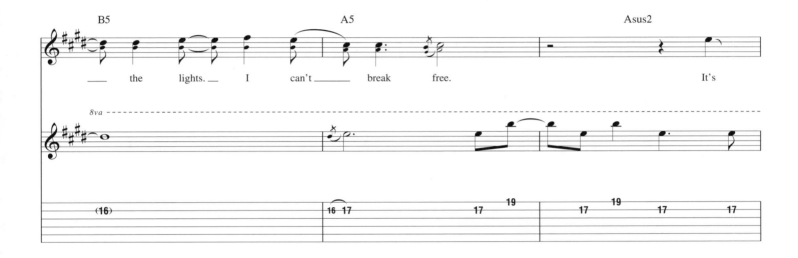

___ the lights. ___ I can't ___ break free. It's

hap - pi - ness ___ or mis - er - y. ___

Gtr. 3

Gtrs. 1 & 4

Harp Solo
Half-time feel
Gtr. 3 tacet
A5
Sure.
Gtrs. 1 & 4
w/ wah-wah
E5
A5
End half-time feel
B7
B7sus4
Gtr. 4
(wah off)
Gtr. 1
(wah off)

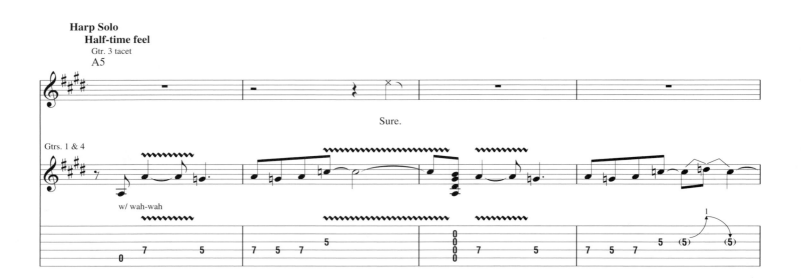

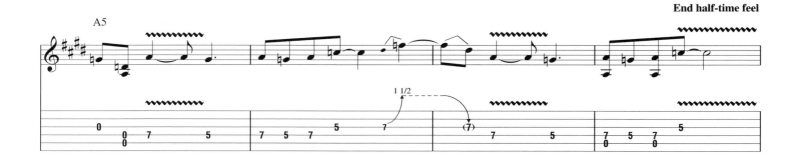

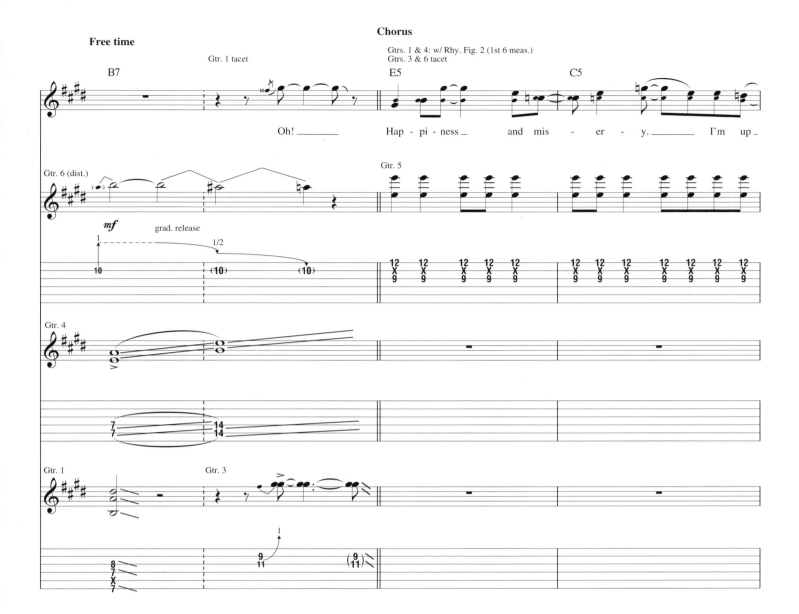

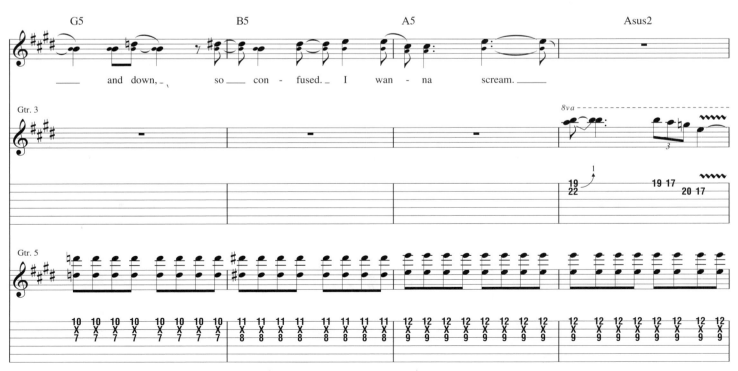

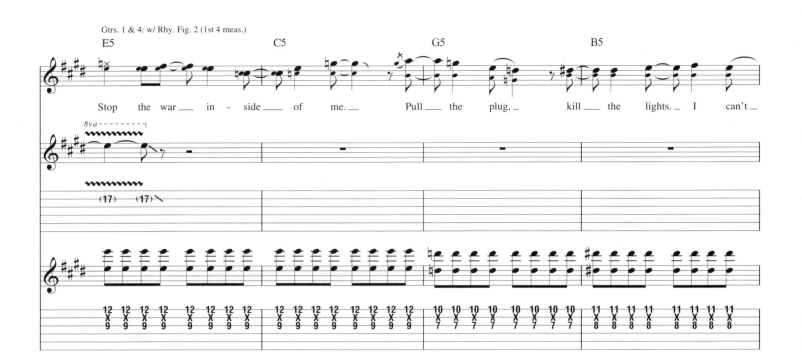

Stop the war in - side — of me. — Pull — the plug, — kill — the lights. — I can't —

Gtr. 5 tacet

— break free. — Hap - pi - ness — or mis - er - y.

Outro-Guitar Solo

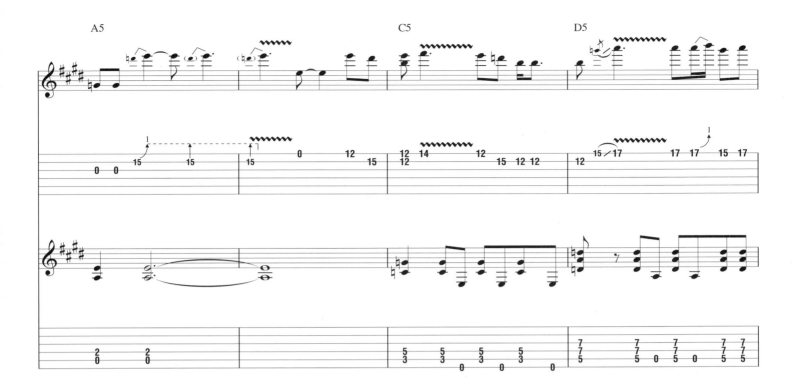

Hide Your Love

Words and Music by Jonny Lang and Marti Frederiksen

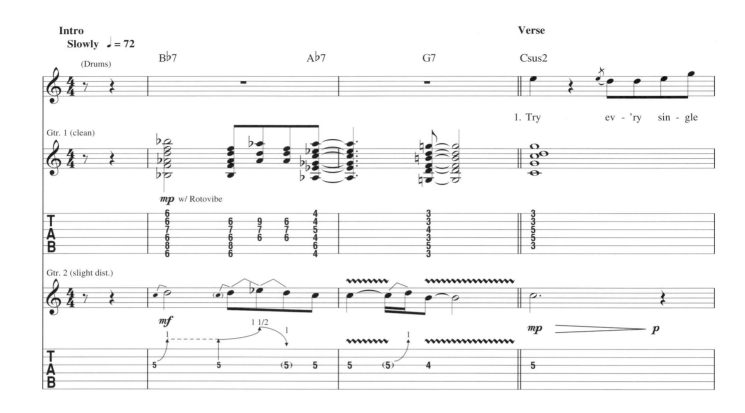

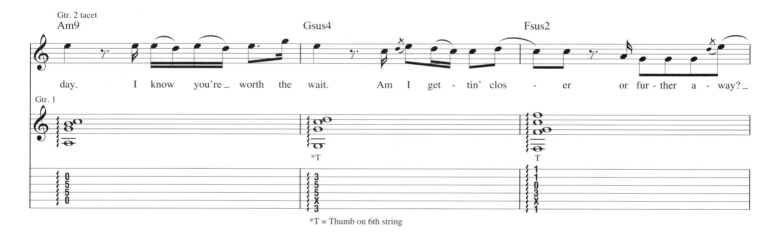

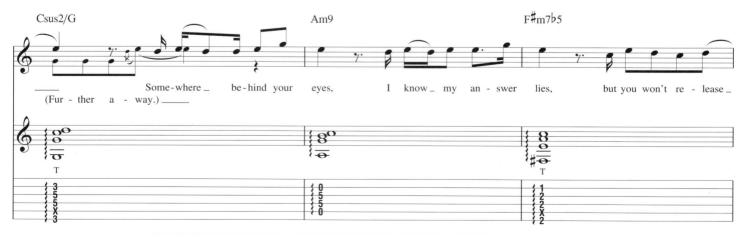

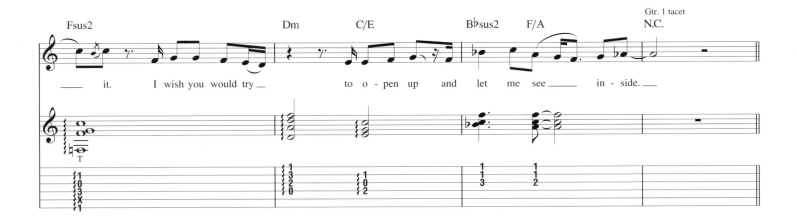

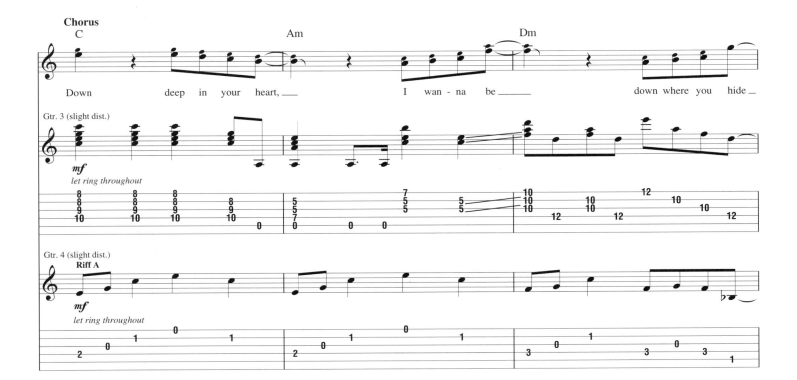

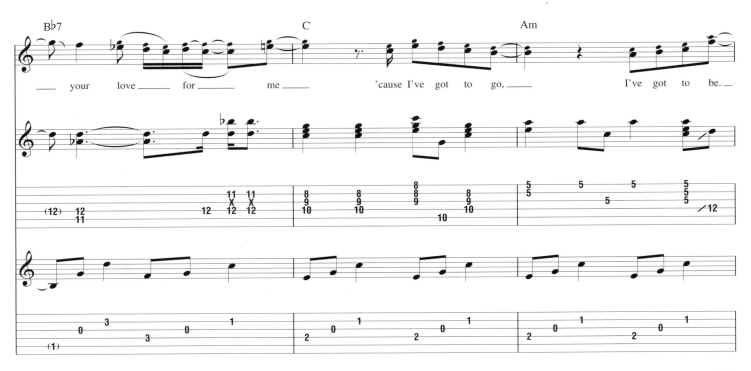

Let me in - side, ___ down where ___ you hide ___ your love ___ for ___ me. ___

Verse

_____ 2. Well, round and round we go, cir - cles all I know, ___ deep - er ___ and deep-

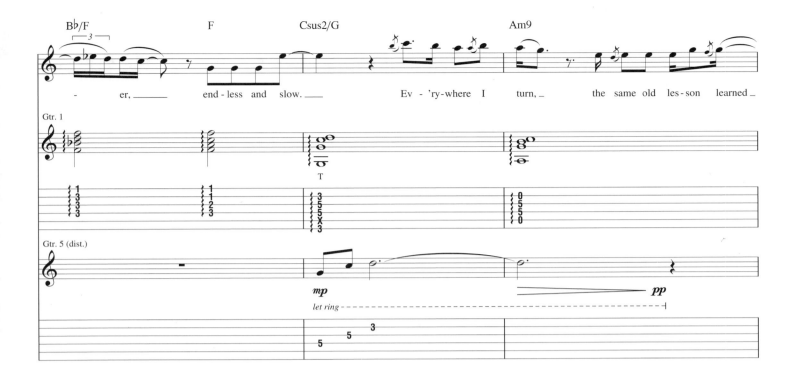

-er, _____ end-less and slow. _____ Ev-'ry-where I turn, _____ the same old les-son learned _____

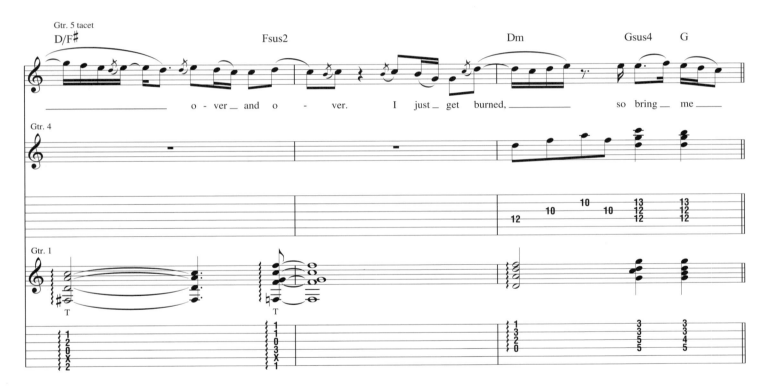

_____ o-ver _ and o - ver. I just _ get burned, _____ so bring _ me _____

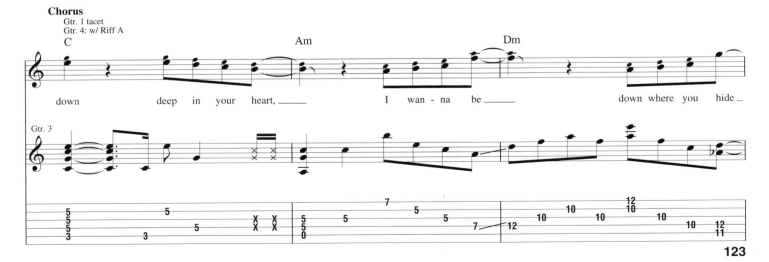

down   deep in your heart, _____ I wan-na be _____ down where you hide _

your love ___ for ___ me ___ 'cause I've got to go, ___ I've got to be. ___

Gtr. 2: w/ Riff B

Let me in - side, ___ down where ___ you hide ___ your love ___ for ___ me, ___

Gtr. 5

Gtr. 3

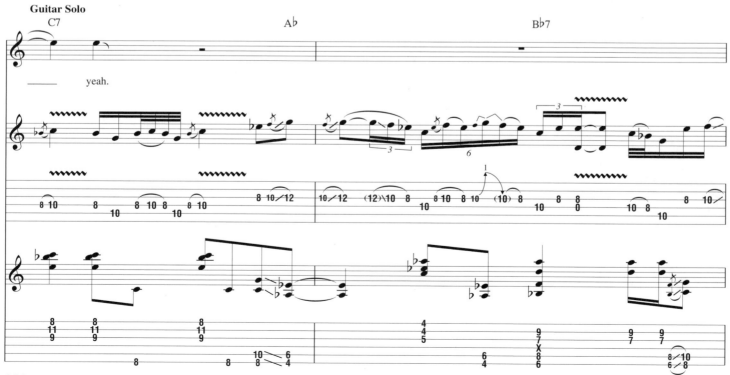

Guitar Solo

___ yeah.

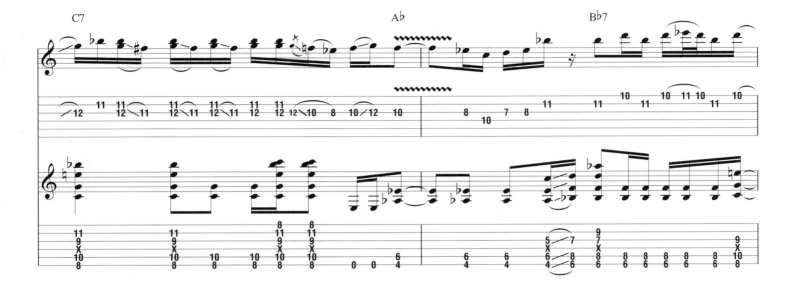

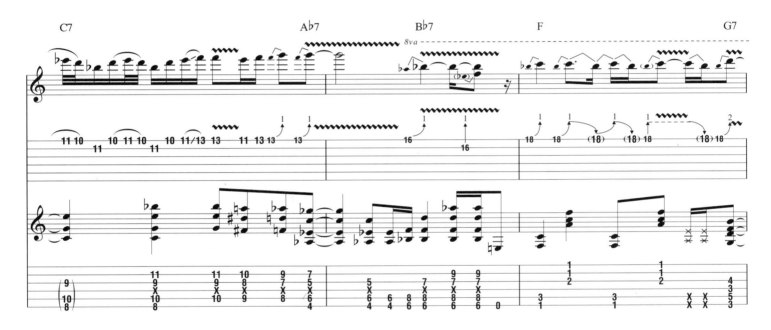

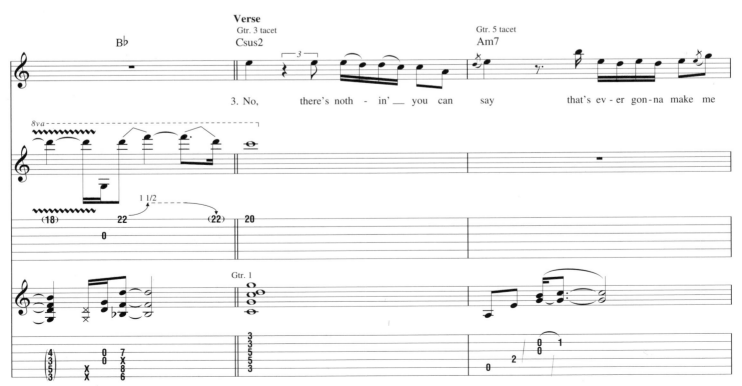

3. No,   there's noth - in' __ you can   say   that's ev - er gon-na make me

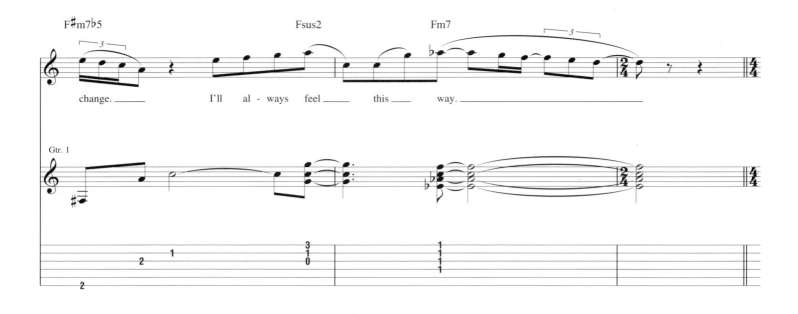

change._____ I'll al - ways feel _____ this _____ way._____

Chorus

Down   deep   in ___ your ___ heart, _____ I wan - na be _____ down where you hide __

___ your   love ___ for _____ me _____ 'cause I've got to go, _____ I've got to be __

down where you hide your love for me.

Outro-Guitar Solo

Gtr. 4: w/ Riff A

w/ Lead Voc. ad lib. (till fade)

C　　Am　　Dm

(Down.

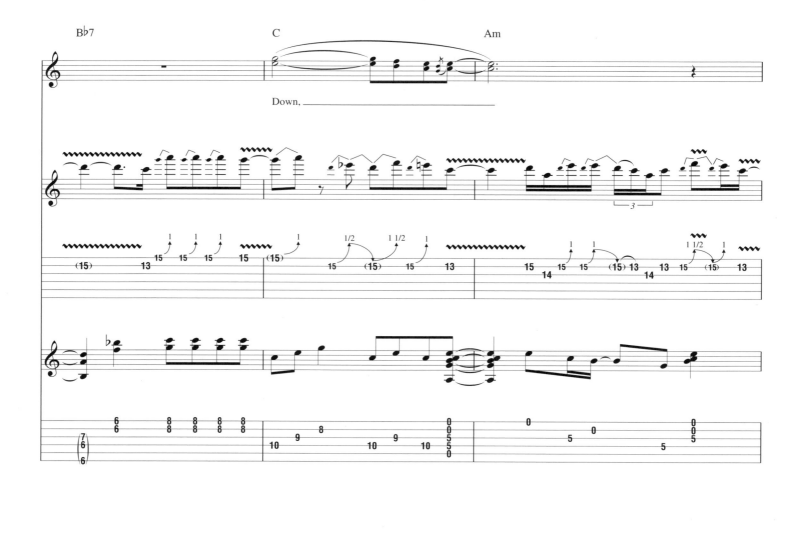

Down, _____

down.) _____

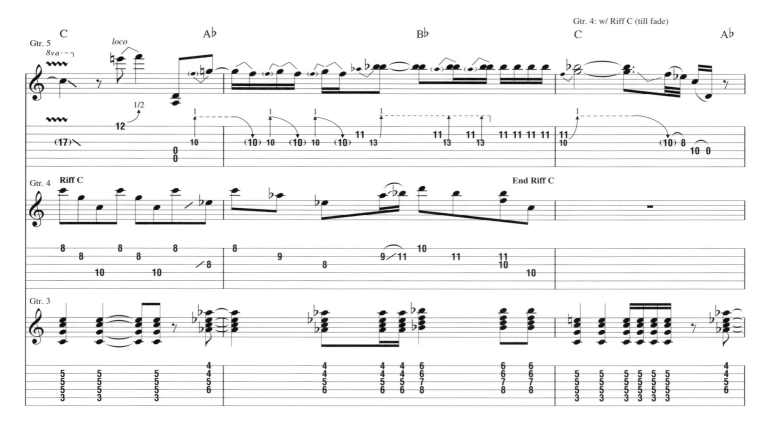

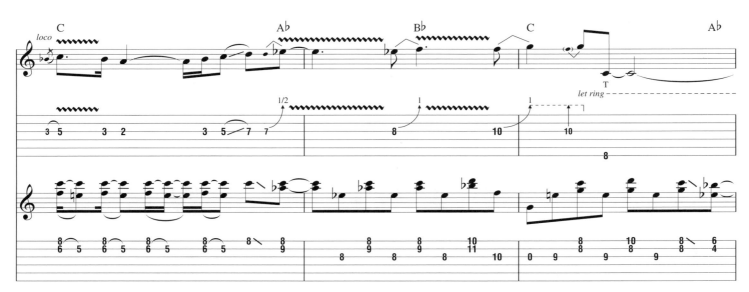

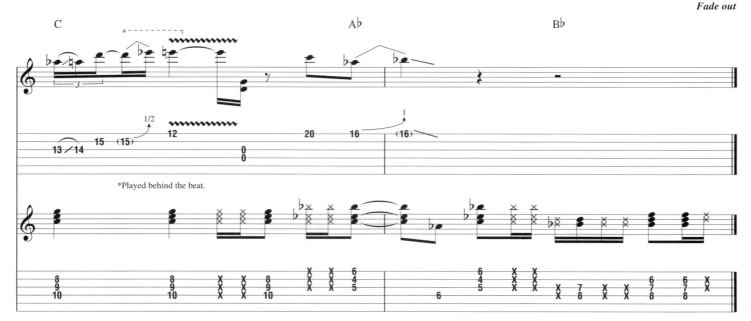

Dying to Live

Words and Music by Edgar Winter

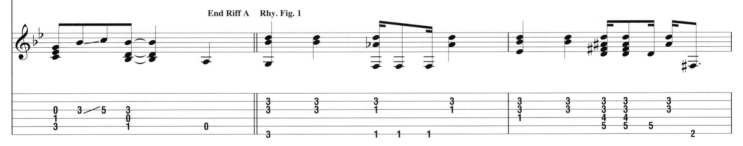

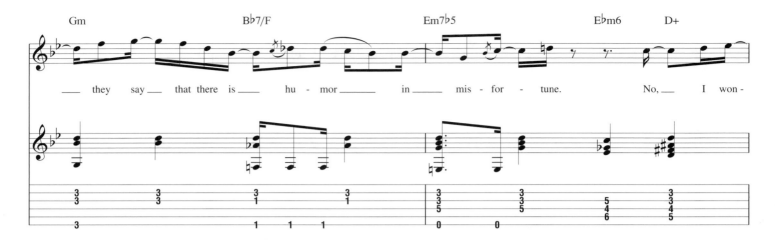

they say — that there is — hu - mor — in — mis - for - tune. No, — I won-

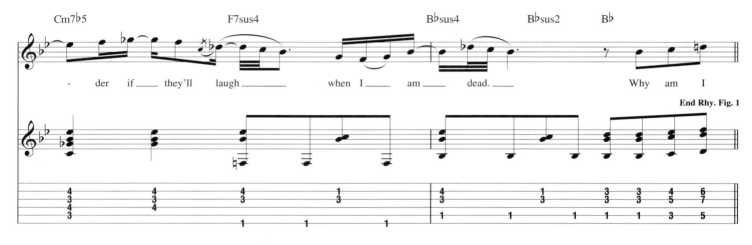

- der if — they'll laugh — when I — am — dead. — Why am I

End Rhy. Fig. 1

𝄋 **Chorus**

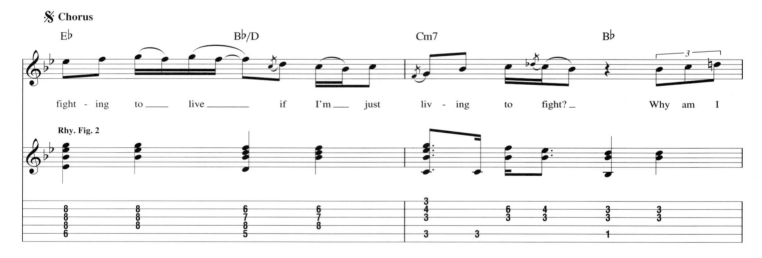

fight - ing to — live — if I'm — just liv - ing to fight? — Why am I

Rhy. Fig. 2

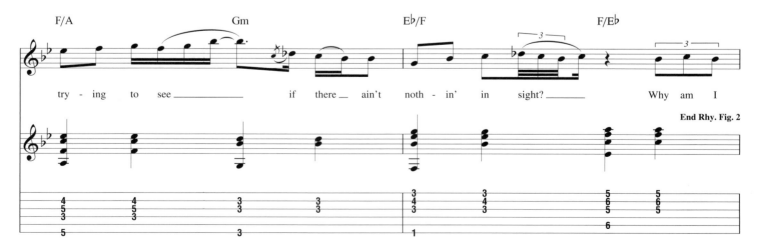

try - ing to see — if there — ain't noth - in' in sight? — Why am I

End Rhy. Fig. 2

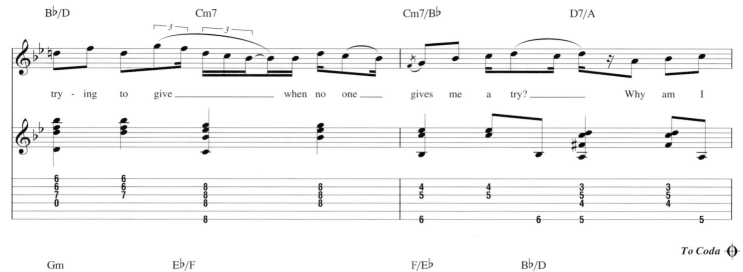

try-ing to give _____ when no one _____ gives me a try? _____ Why am I

To Coda ⊕

dy-ing to _____ live _____ if I'm _____ just liv-ing to die? _____

Interlude
Gtr. 1: w/ Riff A

Oo, _____

Gtr. 2 (slight dist.)

mf

Verse
Gtr. 1: w/ Rhy. Fig. 1

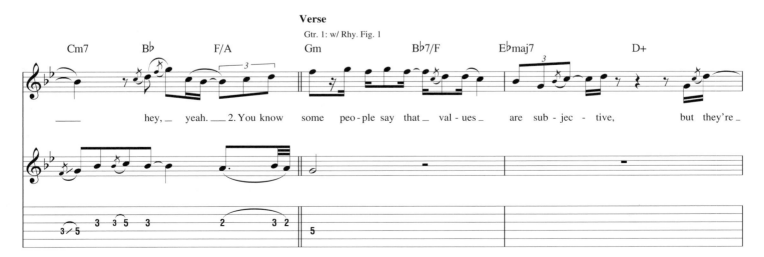

hey, _____ yeah. _____ 2. You know some peo-ple say that _____ val-ues _____ are sub-jec-tive, but they're _____

133

just speak-ing words _____ that some - one else has said. _____ And so ____

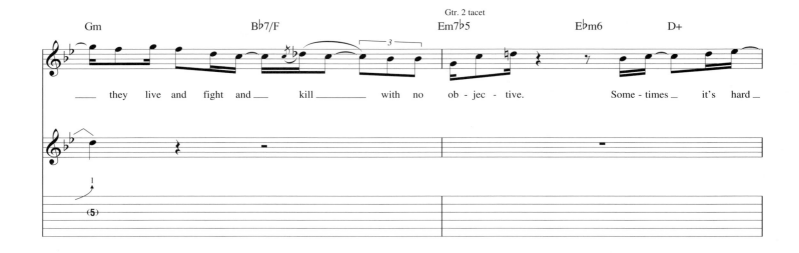

they live and fight and ____ kill _____ with no ob - jec - tive. Some - times ____ it's hard ____

D.S. al Coda

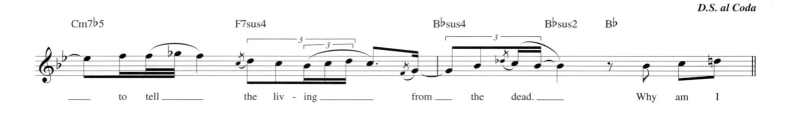

____ to tell _____ the liv - ing _____ from ____ the dead. _____ Why am I

⊕ Coda

Interlude

Gtr. 1: w/ Riff A

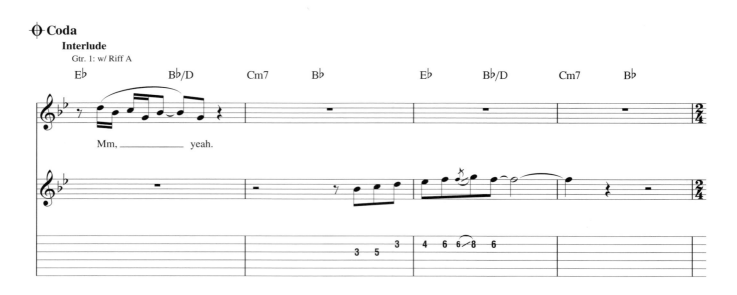

Mm, _____ yeah.

134

Verse

Gtr. 1: w/ Rhy. Fig. 1

3. You know I used to weave my words ___ in - to con - fu - sion, and

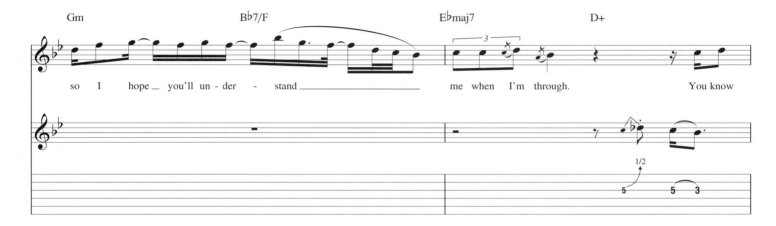

so I hope ___ you'll un - der - stand _____ me when I'm through. You know

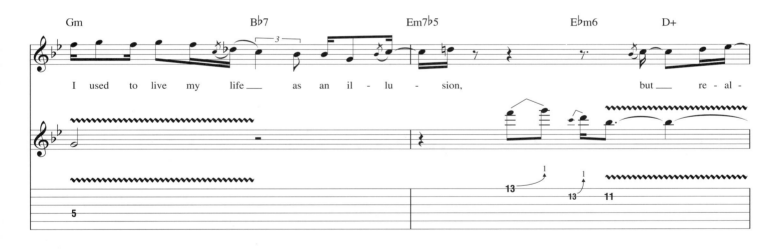

I used to live my life ___ as an il - lu - sion, but ___ re - al -

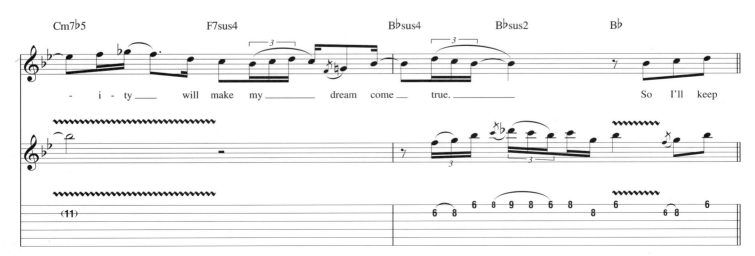

- i - ty ___ will make my dream come ___ true. _____ So I'll keep

Chorus

Gtr. 1: w/ Rhy. Fig. 2

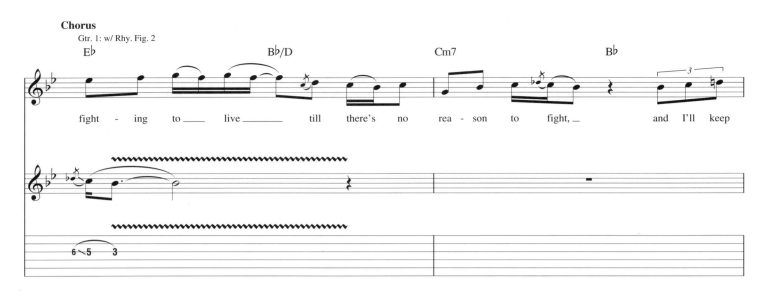

fight - ing to ___ live _____ till there's no rea - son to fight, ___ and I'll keep

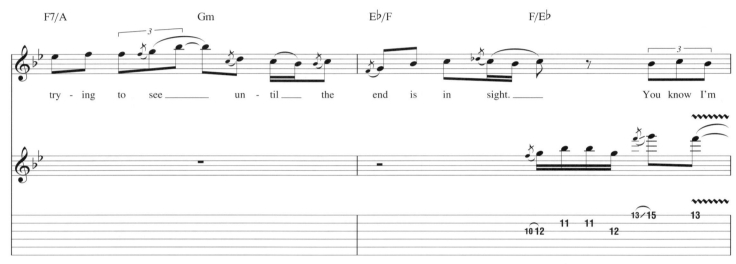

try - ing to see ____ un - til ___ the end is in sight. ____ You know I'm

Rubato

Gtr. 2 tacet

try - ing to give, _____ so come on, _____ give me a try. _____ You know I'm

*Chord symbols reflect overall harmony.

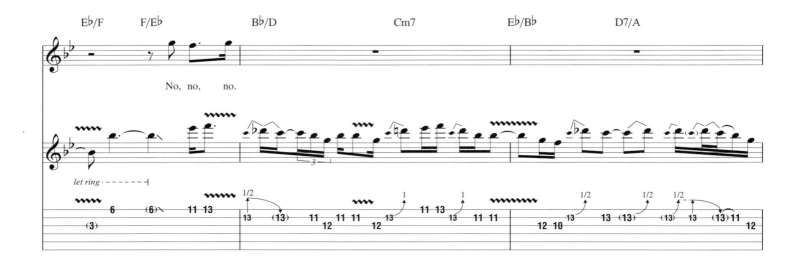

No, no,   no.

Outro
Gtr. 1: w/ Riff A (1st meas.)

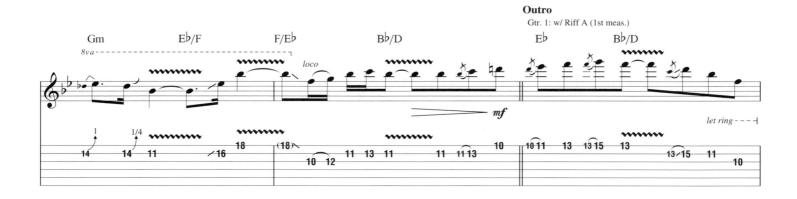

You know I'm   try - ing   to __ live _____ un - til   I'm   rea - dy   to   die. __

Gtr. 2

Gtr. 1

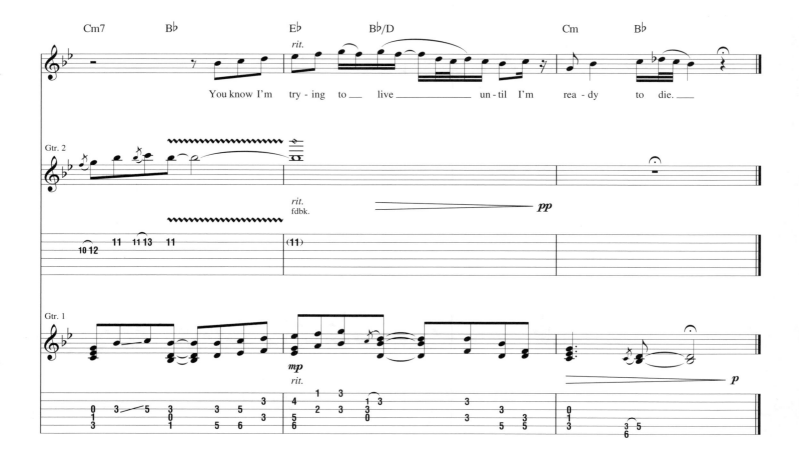

Long Time Coming

Words and Music by Jonny Lang and Marti Frederiksen

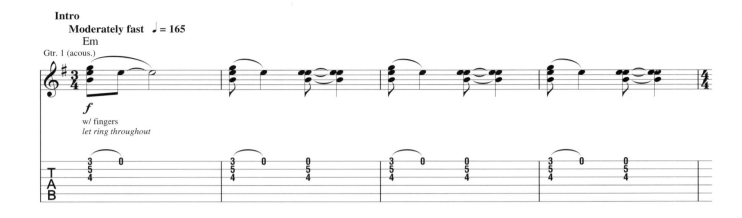

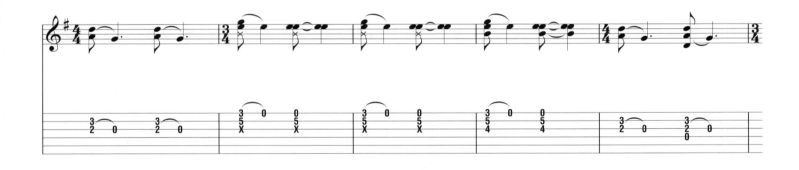

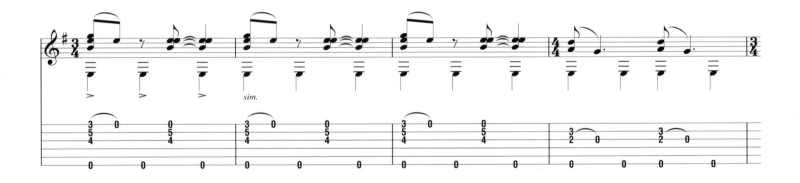

Verse

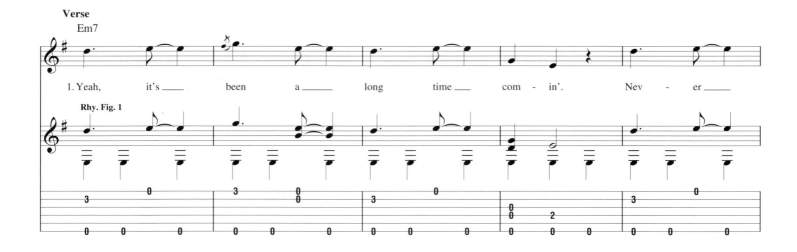

1. Yeah, it's ___ been a ___ long time ___ com - in'. Nev - er ___

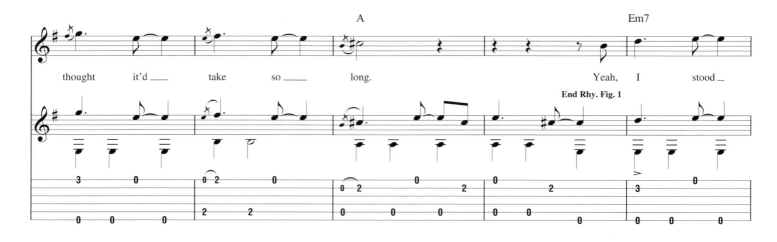

thought it'd ___ take so ___ long. Yeah, I stood ___

still, but ___ time kept ___ run - nin'. Time has ___

Interlude

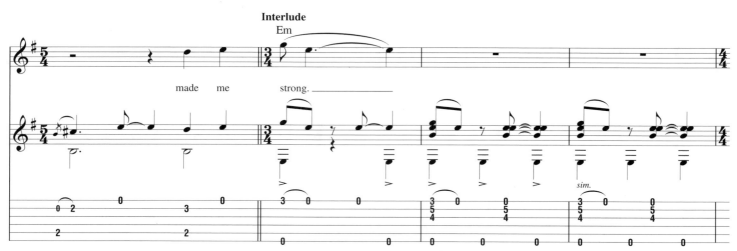

made me strong. ___

Verse
Gtr. 1: w/ Rhy. Fig. 1

Do, do, do, ba, dow,__ de.

2. Time   it's ____ been   a ____ long   time ____ wait - in',

wait - ing ____ for   this ____ day   to ____ come.   And

time   don't ____ wait,   so ____ I   keep ____ sing - in'.

Gtr. 1

Guitar Solo

Do, do, do, do, do, do, da, do, _____ do, ___ do.

Oo, ___ ray, ___ de, din, _____ do, do, da, de, de,

do. Uhn, doy, doy, do, do, do, do, do, do,

do, do, do, ___ do. Do, do, do, do, do, do. De,

Verse
Gtr. 1: w/ Rhy. Fig. 1
Em7

da, de, do, day, ___ do. 3. Yeah, ___ it's ___ been a ___ long time ___ com - in'.

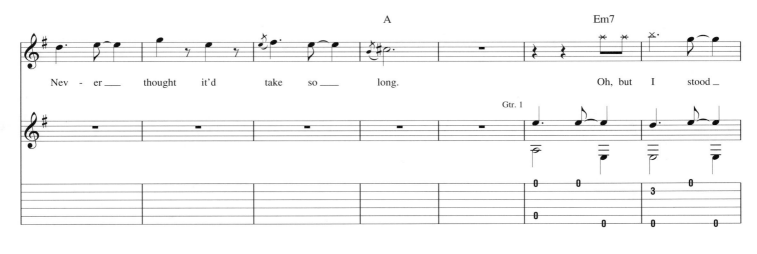

A   Em7

Nev - er ___ thought it'd take so ___ long.   Oh, but I stood ___

Gtr. 1

still and ___ time kept ___ run - nin'.   And time has, _____

uh, _____ made me strong, _____

A5

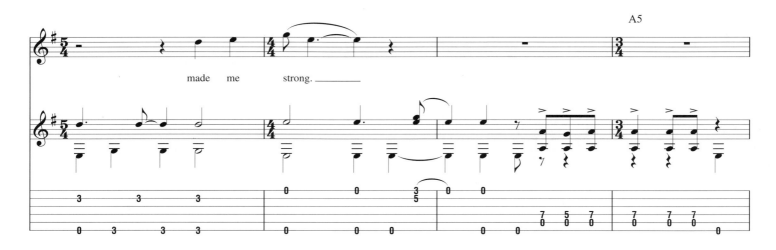

made me strong. _____

G5   Em

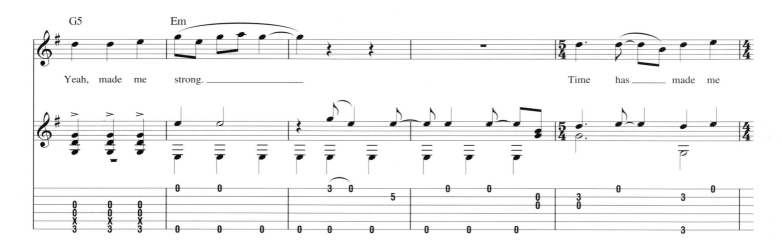

Yeah, made me strong. _____   Time has _____ made me

Free time

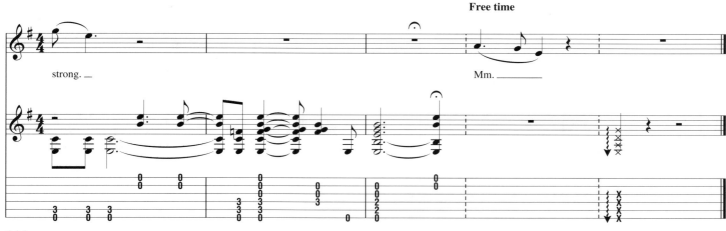

strong. _____   Mm. _____

Living for the City

Words and Music by Stevie Wonder

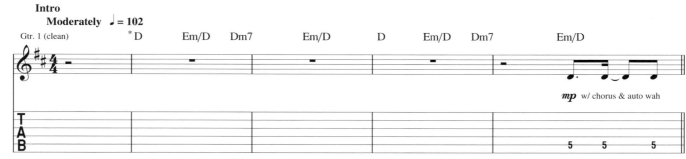

*Chord symbols reflect overall harmony.

to keep him strong, _____ move him in the right _ di - rec - tion. Liv - in'

Chorus

just e - nough, _____ just _____ e - nough _____ for the cit - y. _____

Verse

_____ Yeah. 2. His fa - ther works, _ huh, some days for four-teen hours. _____

And you can bet ___ he bare - ly makes a dol - lar. His moth - er goes ___ to scrub ___

___ the floors ___ for man - y, ___ and you best be - lieve ___ she hard - ly gets ___ a pen - ny. Liv - in'

End Rhy. Fig. 2

let ring - - - - - - - -

P.M. - -

Chorus

Gtr. 2: w/ Rhy. Fig. 1

just e - nough, __ just __ e - nough __ for the cit - y, _____ hey. Na, na, na,

Interlude

Gtr. 1 tacet

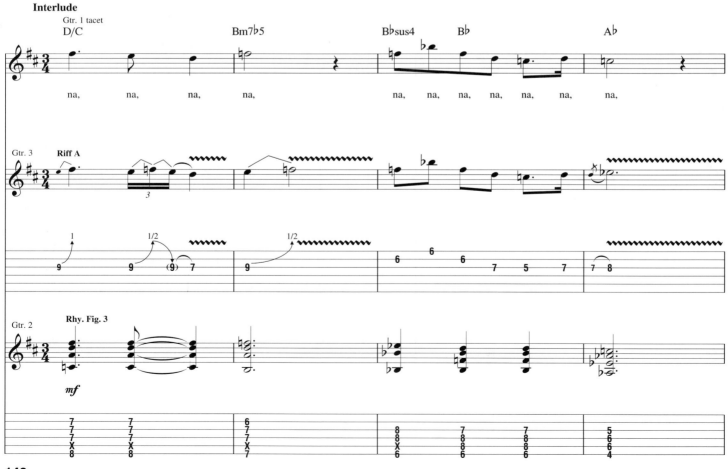

na, na, na, na, na, na, na, na, na, na, na,

na, na, na, na, na, na, na, na, na, _____ uh.

End Riff A

pp

End Rhy. Fig. 3

let ring - - - - - - - - - - - -

Verse

Gtr. 2: w/ Rhy. Fig. 2
Gtr. 3 tacet

3. Well, his sis-ter's black, __ but she is sho' 'nuff pret-ty. _____ Her skirt is short, __ but

Gtr. 1

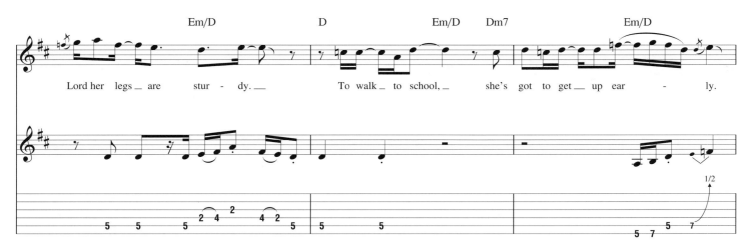

Lord her legs __ are stur-dy. __ To walk __ to school, __ she's got to get __ up ear - ly.

1/2

Chorus

Gtr. 2: w/ Rhy. Fig. 1

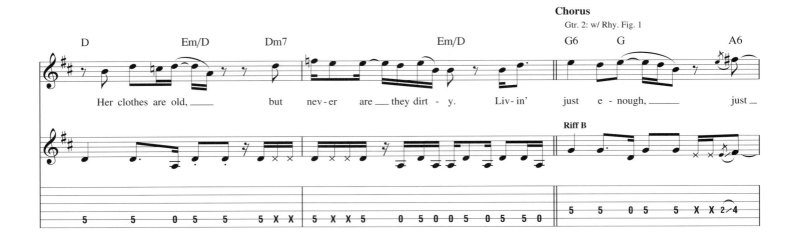

Her clothes are old, ____ but nev-er are ____ they dirt - y. Liv-in' just e - nough, ____ just ____

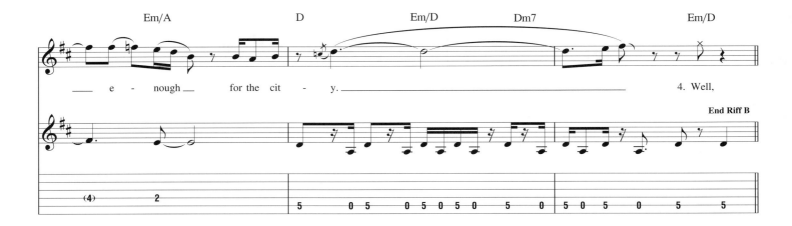

____ e - nough ____ for the cit - y. ____ 4. Well,

Verse

Gtr. 2: w/ Rhy. Fig. 2

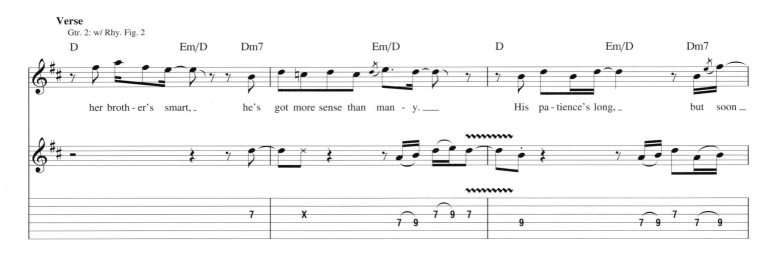

her broth-er's smart, ___ he's got more sense than man - y. ____ His pa-tience's long, __ but soon __

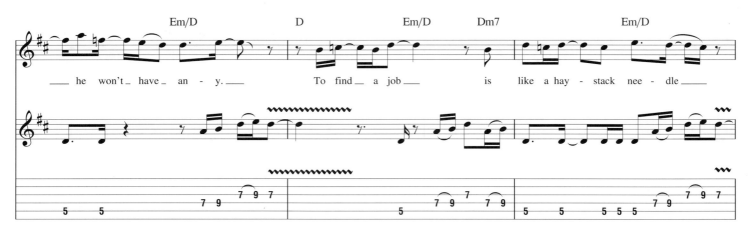

____ he won't __ have __ an - y. ____ To find ___ a job ____ is like a hay - stack nee - dle

Chorus

Gtr. 1: w/ Riff B
Gtr. 2: w/ Rhy. Fig. 1

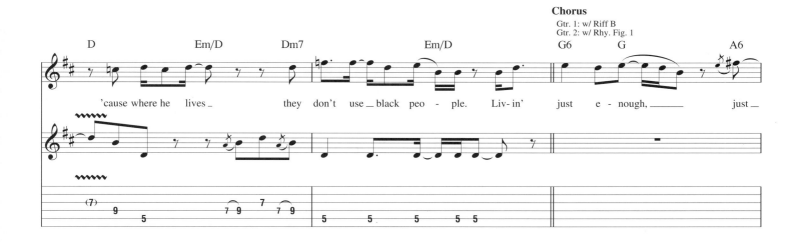

'cause where he lives __ they don't use __ black peo - ple. Liv - in' just e - nough, _____ just __

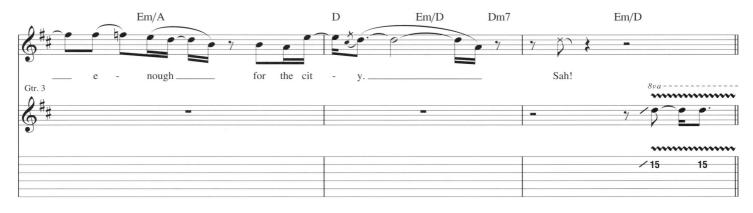

__ e - nough _____ for the cit - y. _____ Sah!

Gtr. 3

Guitar Solo

Gtr. 2: w/ Rhy. Fig. 2

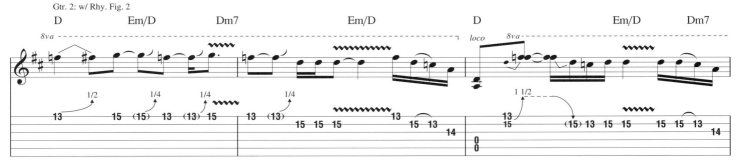

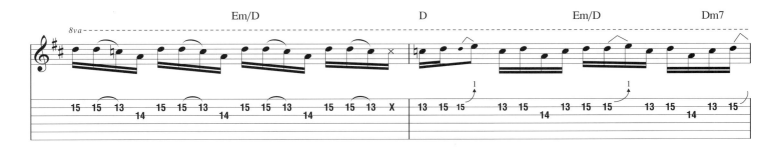

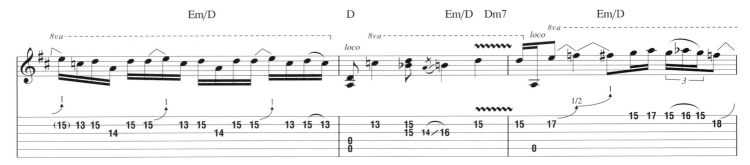

151

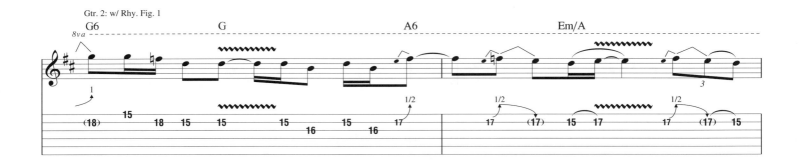

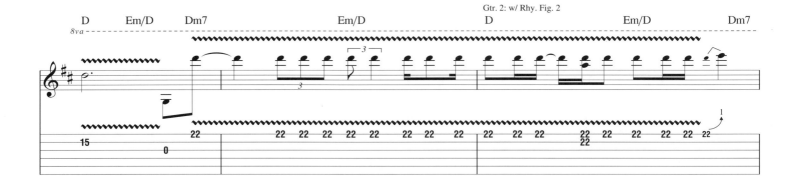

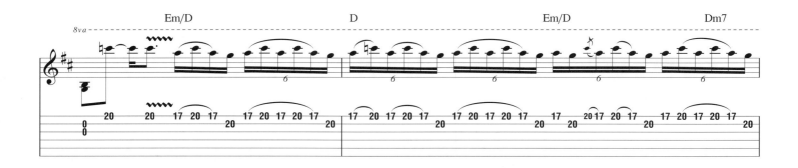

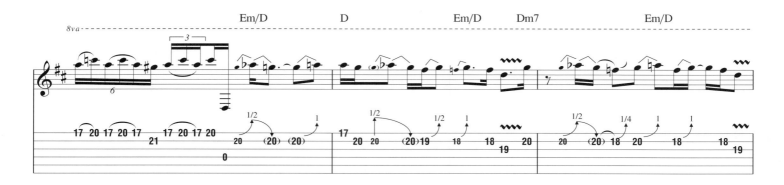

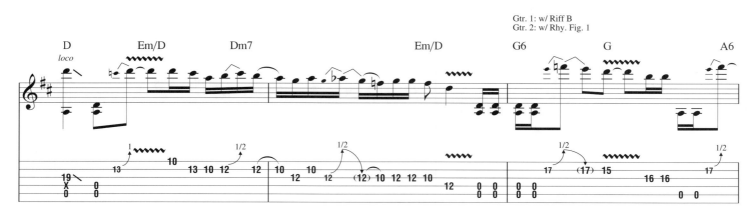

Interlude

Gtr. 2: w/ Rhy. Fig. 3
Gtr. 3: w/ Riff A

Na, na, na,

na, na, na, na, na, na, na, na, na, na, na,

na, na, na, na, na, na, na, na.

Outro

Gtr. 2: w/ Rhy. Fig. 2 (2 times)

Liv - in' just e - nough for the cit - y, oh.

Voc. Fig. 1

(Liv - in' just e - nough for the cit - y, oh.

Liv - in' just e - nough for the cit - y. Well,

End Voc. Fig. 1

Liv - in' just e - nough for the cit - y. oh.)

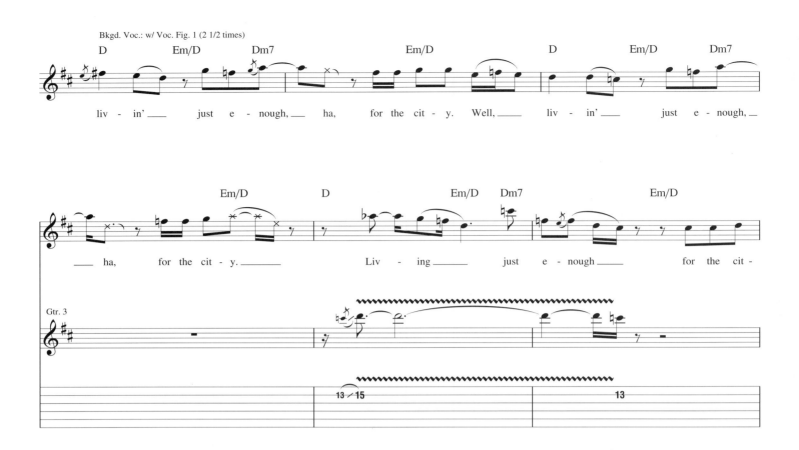

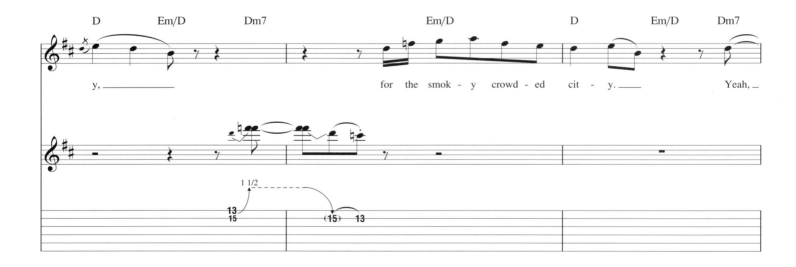

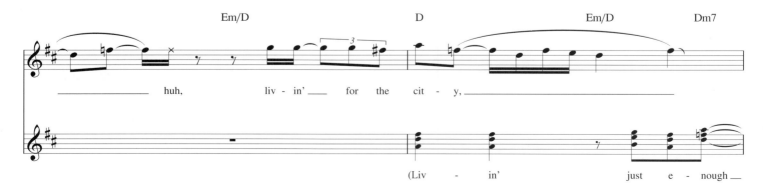

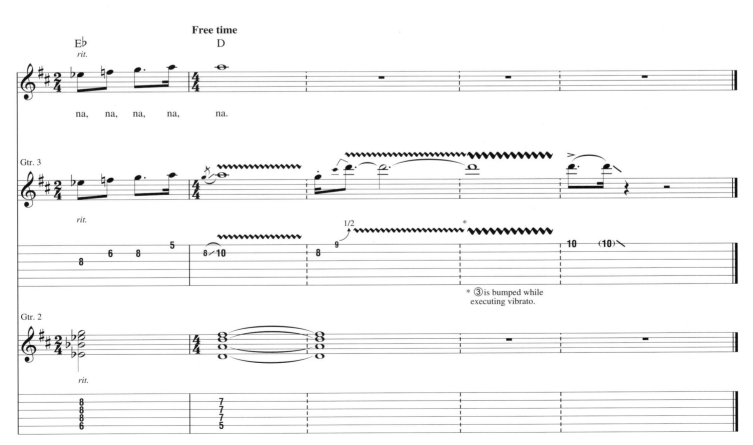

Guitar Notation Legend

Guitar Music can be notated three different ways: on a *musical staff*, in *tablature*, and in *rhythm slashes*.

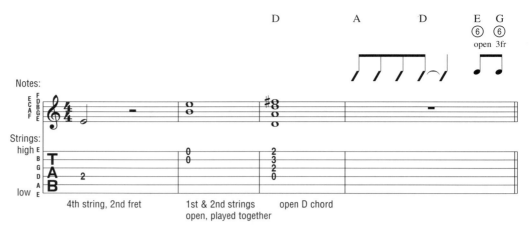

RHYTHM SLASHES are written above the staff. Strum chords in the rhythm indicated. Use the chord diagrams found at the top of the first page of the transcription for the appropriate chord voicings. Round noteheads indicate single notes.

THE MUSICAL STAFF shows pitches and rhythms and is divided by bar lines into measures. Pitches are named after the first seven letters of the alphabet.

TABLATURE graphically represents the guitar fingerboard. Each horizontal line represents a a string, and each number represents a fret.

4th string, 2nd fret

1st & 2nd strings open, played together

open D chord

Definitions for Special Guitar Notation

HALF-STEP BEND: Strike the note and bend up 1/2 step.

WHOLE-STEP BEND: Strike the note and bend up one step.

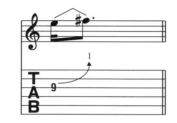

GRACE NOTE BEND: Strike the note and immediately bend up as indicated.

SLIGHT (MICROTONE) BEND: Strike the note and bend up 1/4 step.

BEND AND RELEASE: Strike the note and bend up as indicated, then release back to the original note. Only the first note is struck.

PRE-BEND: Bend the note as indicated, then strike it.

PRE-BEND AND RELEASE: Bend the note as indicated. Strike it and release the bend back to the original note.

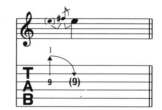

UNISON BEND: Strike the two notes simultaneously and bend the lower note up to the pitch of the higher.

VIBRATO: The string is vibrated by rapidly bending and releasing the note with the fretting hand.

WIDE VIBRATO: The pitch is varied to a greater degree by vibrating with the fretting hand.

HAMMER-ON: Strike the first (lower) note with one finger, then sound the higher note (on the same string) with another finger by fretting it without picking.

PULL-OFF: Place both fingers on the notes to be sounded. Strike the first note and without picking, pull the finger off to sound the second (lower) note.

LEGATO SLIDE: Strike the first note and then slide the same fret-hand finger up or down to the second note. The second note is not struck.

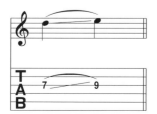

SHIFT SLIDE: Same as legato slide, except the second note is struck.

TRILL: Very rapidly alternate between the notes indicated by continuously hammering on and pulling off.

TAPPING: Hammer ("tap") the fret indicated with the pick-hand index or middle finger and pull off to the note fretted by the fret hand.

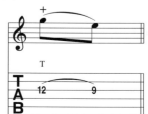

NATURAL HARMONIC: Strike the note while the fret-hand lightly touches the string directly over the fret indicated.

Harm.

PINCH HARMONIC: The note is fretted normally and a harmonic is produced by adding the edge of the thumb or the tip of the index finger of the pick hand to the normal pick attack.

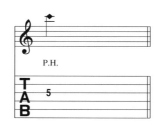

P.H.

HARP HARMONIC: The note is fretted normally and a harmonic is produced by gently resting the pick hand's index finger directly above the indicated fret (in parentheses) while the pick hand's thumb or pick assists by plucking the appropriate string.

H.H.

PICK SCRAPE: The edge of the pick is rubbed down (or up) the string, producing a scratchy sound.

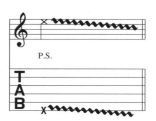

P.S.

MUFFLED STRINGS: A percussive sound is produced by laying the fret hand across the string(s) without depressing, and striking them with the pick hand.

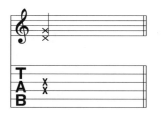

PALM MUTING: The note is partially muted by the pick hand lightly touching the string(s) just before the bridge.

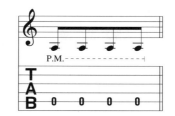

P.M.

RAKE: Drag the pick across the strings indicated with a single motion.

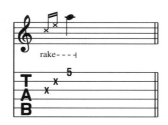

rake

TREMOLO PICKING: The note is picked as rapidly and continuously as possible.

ARPEGGIATE: Play the notes of the chord indicated by quickly rolling them from bottom to top.

VIBRATO BAR DIVE AND RETURN: The pitch of the note or chord is dropped a specified number of steps (in rhythm) then returned to the original pitch.

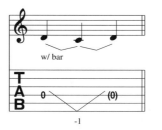

w/ bar

VIBRATO BAR SCOOP: Depress the bar just before striking the note, then quickly release the bar.

w/ bar

VIBRATO BAR DIP: Strike the note and then immediately drop a specified number of steps, then release back to the original pitch.

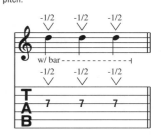

w/ bar

Additional Musical Definitions

> (accent)	• Accentuate note (play it louder)	
^ (accent)	• Accentuate note with great intensity	
• (staccato)	• Play the note short	
⊓	• Downstroke	
V	• Upstroke	
D.S. al Coda	• Go back to the sign (𝄋), then play until the measure marked "**To Coda**," then skip to the section labelled "**Coda**."	
D.C. al Fine	• Go back to the beginning of the song and play until the measure marked "**Fine**" (end).	

Rhy. Fig.	• Label used to recall a recurring accompaniment pattern (usually chordal).
Riff	• Label used to recall composed, melodic lines (usually single notes) which recur.
Fill	• Label used to identify a brief melodic figure which is to be inserted into the arrangement.
Rhy. Fill	• A chordal version of a Fill.
tacet	• Instrument is silent (drops out).
	• Repeat measures between signs.
1. ‖ 2.	• When a repeated section has different endings, play the first ending only the first time and the second ending only the second time.

NOTE: Tablature numbers in parentheses mean:
1. The note is being sustained over a system (note in standard notation is tied), or
2. The note is sustained, but a new articulation (such as a hammer-on, pull-off, slide or vibrato begins), or
3. The note is a barely audible "ghost" note (note in standard notation is also in parentheses).

RECORDED VERSIONS
The Best Note-For-Note Transcriptions Available

ALL BOOKS INCLUDE TABLATURE

00690501	Adams, Bryan – Greatest Hits $19.95
00692015	Aerosmith – Greatest Hits $22.95
00690178	Alice in Chains – Acoustic $19.95
00690387	Alice in Chains – Nothing Safe:
	The Best of the Box $19.95
00694932	Allman Brothers Band – Volume 1 . . . . . .$24.95
00694933	Allman Brothers Band – Volume 2 . . . . . .$24.95
00694878	Atkins, Chet – Vintage Fingerstyle $19.95
00690418	Audio Adrenaline, Best of $17.95
00690609	Audioslave $19.95
00690366	Bad Company – Original Anthology, Book 1 . .$19.95
00690503	Beach Boys – Very Best of $19.95
00690489	Beatles – 1 . . . .$24.95
00694929	Beatles – 1962-1966 . . . .$24.95
00694930	Beatles – 1967-1970 . . . .$24.95
00694832	Beatles – For Acoustic Guitar $19.95
00690137	Beatles – A Hard Day's Night $16.95
00690482	Beatles – Let It Be $16.95
00690632	Beck – Sea Change $19.95
00694884	Benson, George – Best of $19.95
00692385	Berry, Chuck $19.95
00692200	Black Sabbath –
	We Sold Our Soul for Rock 'N' Roll $19.95
00690674	Blink-182 . . . .$19.95
00690389	Blink-182 – Enema of the State $19.95
00690523	Blink-182 – Take Off Your Pants & Jacket .$19.95
00690028	Blue Oyster Cult – Cult Classics $19.95
00690583	Boxcar Racer $19.95
00690491	Bowie, David – Best of $19.95
00690451	Buckley, Jeff – Collection $24.95
00690364	Cake – Songbook $19.95
00690564	Calling, The – Camino Palmero $29.95
00690043	Cheap Trick – Best of $19.95
00690567	Christian, Charlie – Definitive Collection . .$19.95
00690590	Clapton, Eric – Anthology $29.95
00692391	Clapton, Eric – Best of, 2nd Edition $22.95
00690415	Clapton Chronicles – Best of Eric Clapton .$18.95
00690074	Clapton, Eric – The Cream of Clapton $24.95
00694869	Clapton, Eric – Unplugged $22.95
00690162	Clash, Best of The $19.95
00690494	Coldplay – Parachutes $19.95
00690593	Coldplay – A Rush of Blood to the Head . .$19.95
00694940	Counting Crows – August & Everything After $19.95
00690401	Creed – Human Clay $19.95
00690352	Creed – My Own Prison $19.95
00690551	Creed – Weathered $19.95
00699521	Cure, The – Greatest Hits $24.95
00690484	dc Talk – Intermission: The Greatest Hits .$19.95
00690289	Deep Purple, Best of $17.95
00690563	Default – The Fallout $19.95
00690384	Di Franco, Ani – Best of $19.95
00695382	Dire Straits – Sultans of Swing $19.95
00690347	Doors, The – Anthology $22.95
00690348	Doors, The – Essential Guitar Collection . . .$16.95
00690555	Etheridge, Melissa – Best of $19.95
00690524	Etheridge, Melissa – Skin $19.95
00690515	Extreme II – Pornograffitti $19.95
00690235	Foo Fighters – The Colour and the Shape .$19.95
00690595	Foo Fighters – One by One $19.95
00690394	Foo Fighters –
	There Is Nothing Left to Lose $19.95
00690222	G3 Live – Satriani, Vai, Johnson $22.95
00690338	Goo Goo Dolls – Dizzy Up the Girl $19.95
00690576	Goo Goo Dolls – Gutterflower $19.95

00690601	Good Charlotte –
	The Young and the Hopeless $19.95
00690591	Griffin, Patty – Guitar Collection $19.95
00694798	Harrison, George – Anthology $19.95
00692930	Hendrix, Jimi – Are You Experienced? $24.95
00692931	Hendrix, Jimi – Axis: Bold As Love $22.95
00690017	Hendrix, Jimi – Live at Woodstock $24.95
00690602	Hendrix, Jimi – Smash Hits $19.95
00660029	Holly, Buddy $19.95
00690457	Incubus – Make Yourself $19.95
00690544	Incubus – Morningview $19.95
00690136	Indigo Girls – 1200 Curfews $22.95
00694912	Johnson, Eric – Ah Via Musicom $19.95
00690660	Johnson, Eric – Best of $19.95
00690271	Johnson, Robert – New Transcriptions . . .$24.95
00699131	Joplin, Janis – Best of $19.95
00690427	Judas Priest – Best of $19.95
00690504	King, Albert – The Very Best of $19.95
00690444	King, B.B. and Eric Clapton –
	Riding with the King $19.95
00690339	Kinks, The – Best of $19.95
00690614	Lavigne, Avril – Let Go $19.95
00690525	Lynch, George – Best of $19.95
00694755	Malmsteen, Yngwie – Rising Force $19.95
00694956	Marley, Bob – Legend $19.95
00690548	Marley, Bob – One Love: Very Best of $19.95
00694945	Marley, Bob – Songs of Freedom $24.95
00690616	Matchbox 20 – More Than You Think You Are .$19.95
00690239	Matchbox 20 – Yourself or Someone Like You .$19.95
00690382	McLachlan, Sarah – Mirrorball $19.95
00694952	Megadeth – Countdown to Extinction $19.95
00694951	Megadeth – Rust in Peace $22.95
00690495	Megadeth – The World Needs a Hero $19.95
00690505	Mellencamp, John – Guitar Collection $19.95
00690562	Metheny, Pat – Bright Size Life $19.95
00690559	Metheny, Pat – Question and Answer $19.95
00690611	Nirvana $22.95
00690189	Nirvana – From the Muddy
	Banks of the Wishkah $19.95
00694913	Nirvana – In Utero $19.95
00694883	Nirvana – Nevermind $19.95
00690026	Nirvana – Unplugged in New York $19.95
00690121	Oasis – (What's the Story) Morning Glory . .$19.95
00690358	Offspring, The – Americana $19.95
00690485	Offspring, The – Conspiracy of One $19.95
00690552	Offspring, The – Ignition $19.95
00690663	Offspring, The – Splinter $19.95
00694847	Osbourne, Ozzy – Best of $22.95
00690547	Osbourne, Ozzy – Down to Earth $19.95
00690399	Osbourne, Ozzy – Ozzman Cometh $19.95
00694855	Pearl Jam – Ten $19.95
00690439	Perfect Circle, A – Mer De Noms $19.95
00690499	Petty, Tom – The Definitive
	Guitar Collection $19.95
00690424	Phish – Farmhouse $19.95
00690240	Phish – Hoist $19.95
00690607	Phish – Round Room $19.95
00690331	Phish – Story of the Ghost $19.95
00690642	Pillar – Fireproof $19.95
00690428	Pink Floyd – Dark Side of the Moon $19.95
00690546	P.O.D. – Satellite $19.95
00693864	Police, The – Best of $19.95
00690299	Presley, Elvis – Best of Elvis:
	The King of Rock 'n' Roll $19.95
00694975	Queen – Greatest Hits $24.95
00694910	Rage Against the Machine $19.95

00690145	Rage Against the Machine – Evil Empire . .$19.95
00690426	Ratt – Best of $19.95
00690055	Red Hot Chili Peppers –
	Bloodsugarsexmagik $19.95
00690584	Red Hot Chili Peppers – By the Way $19.95
00690379	Red Hot Chili Peppers – Californication . . .$19.95
00690090	Red Hot Chili Peppers – One Hot Minute . .$22.95
00690511	Reinhardt, Django – Definitive Collection . .$19.95
00690643	Relient K – Two Lefts Don't
	Make a Right...But Three Do $19.95
00690014	Rolling Stones – Exile on Main Street $24.95
00690631	Rolling Stones – Guitar Anthology $24.95
00690600	Saliva – Back Into Your System $19.95
00690031	Santana's Greatest Hits $19.95
00690566	Scorpions – Best of $19.95
00690604	Seger, Bob – Guitar Collection $19.95
00690419	Slipknot $19.95
00690530	Slipknot – Iowa $19.95
00690385	Sonicflood $19.95
00690021	Sting – Fields of Gold $19.95
00690597	Stone Sour $19.95
00690520	Styx Guitar Collection $19.95
00690519	Sum 41 – All Killer No Filler $19.95
00690612	Sum 41 – Does This Look Infected? $19.95
00690425	System of a Down $19.95
00690606	System of a Down – Steal This Album $19.95
00690531	System of a Down – Toxicity $19.95
00694824	Taylor, James – Best of $16.95
00690238	Third Eye Blind $19.95
00690580	311 – From Chaos $19.95
00690295	Tool – Aenima $19.95
00690654	Train – Best of $19.95
00690039	Vai, Steve – Alien Love Secrets $24.95
00690392	Vai, Steve – The Ultra Zone $19.95
00690370	Vaughan, Stevie Ray and Double Trouble –
	The Real Deal: Greatest Hits Volume 2 .$22.95
00690116	Vaughan, Stevie Ray – Guitar Collection . . .$24.95
00660058	Vaughan, Stevie Ray –
	Lightnin' Blues 1983-1987 . . . .$24.95
00690550	Vaughan, Stevie Ray and Double Trouble –
	Live at Montreux 1982 & 1985 . . . . .$24.95
00694835	Vaughan, Stevie Ray – The Sky Is Crying . .$22.95
00690015	Vaughan, Stevie Ray – Texas Flood $19.95
00694789	Waters, Muddy – Deep Blues $24.95
00690071	Weezer (The Blue Album) $19.95
00690516	Weezer (The Green Album) $19.95
00690579	Weezer – Maladroit $19.95
00690286	Weezer – Pinkerton $19.95
00690447	Who, The – Best of $24.95
00690640	Wilcox, David – Anthology 2000-2003 . . . .$19.95
00690320	Williams, Dar – Best of $17.95
00690596	Yardbirds, The – Best of $19.95
00690443	Zappa, Frank – Hot Rats $19.95
00690589	ZZ Top Guitar Anthology $22.95

INCLUDES TAB

GUITAR PLAY-ALONG

The Guitar Play-Along Series will help you play your favorite songs quickly and easily. Just follow the tab and listen to the CD to hear how the guitar should sound, and then play along using the separate backing tracks. Mac or PC users can also slow down the tempo by using the CD in their computer. The melody and lyrics are also included in the book in case you want to sing, or to simply help you follow along. 8 songs in each book.

VOLUME 1 – ROCK GUITAR
Day Tripper • Message in a Bottle • Refugee • Shattered • Sunshine of Your Love • Takin' Care of Business • Tush • Walk This Way.
_____00699570 Book/CD Pack $12.95

VOLUME 2 – ACOUSTIC GUITAR
Angie • Behind Blue Eyes • Best of My Love • Blackbird • Dust in the Wind • Layla • Night Moves • Yesterday.
_____00699569 Book/CD Pack $12.95

VOLUME 3 – HARD ROCK
Crazy Train • Iron Man • Living After Midnight • Rock You like a Hurricane • Round and Round • Smoke on the Water • Sweet Child O' Mine • You Really Got Me.
_____00699573 Book/CD Pack...........................$14.95

VOLUME 4 – POP/ROCK
Breakdown • Crazy Little Thing Called Love • Hit Me with Your Best Shot • I Want You to Want Me • Lights • R.O.C.K. in the U.S.A. (A Salute to 60's Rock) • Summer of '69 • What I like About You.
_____00699571 Book/CD Pack...........................$12.95

VOLUME 5 – MODERN ROCK
Aerials • Alive • Bother • Chop Suey! • Control • Last Resort • Take a Look Around (Theme from "M:I-2") • Wish You Were Here.
_____00699574 Book/CD Pack...........................$12.95

VOLUME 6 – '90S ROCK
Are You Gonna Go My Way • Come Out and Play • I'll Stick Around • Know Your Enemy • Man in the Box • Outshined • Smells like Teen Spirit • Under the Bridge.
_____00699572 Book/CD Pack...........................$12.95

VOLUME 7 – BLUES GUITAR
All Your Love (I Miss Loving) • Born Under a Bad Sign • Hide Away • I'm Tore Down • I'm Your Hoochie Coochie Man • Pride and Joy • Sweet Home Chicago • The Thrill Is Gone.
_____00699575 Book/CD Pack...........................$12.95

VOLUME 8 – ROCK
All Right Now • Black Magic Woman • Get Back • Hey Joe • Layla • Love Me Two Times • Won't Get Fooled Again • You Really Got Me.
_____00699585 Book/CD Pack...........................$12.95

VOLUME 9 – PUNK ROCK
All the Small Things • Fat Lip • Flavor of the Weak • Hash Pipe • I Feel So • Pretty Fly (For a White Guy) • Say It Ain't So • Self Esteem.
_____00699576 Book/CD Pack...........................$12.95

VOLUME 10 – ACOUSTIC
Have You Ever Really Loved a Woman? • Here Comes the Sun • The Magic Bus • Norwegian Wood (This Bird Has Flown) • Space Oddity • Spanish Caravan • Tangled up in Blue • Tears in Heaven.
_____00699586 Book/CD Pack...........................$12.95

VOLUME 11 – EARLY ROCK
Fun, Fun, Fun • Hound Dog • Louie, Louie • No Particular Place to Go • Oh, Pretty Woman • Rock Around the Clock • Under the Boardwalk • Wild Thing.
_____00699579 Book/CD Pack...........................$12.95

VOLUME 12 – POP/ROCK
Every Breath You Take • I Wish It Would Rain • Money for Nothing • Rebel, Rebel • Run to You • Ticket to Ride • Wonderful Tonight • You Give Love a Bad Name.
_____00699587 Book/CD Pack...........................$12.95

VOLUME 13 – FOLK ROCK
Leaving on a Jet Plane • Suite: Judy Blue Eyes • Take Me Home, Country Roads • This Land Is   Your Land • Time in a Bottle • Turn! Turn! Turn! (To Everything There Is a Season) • You've Got a Friend • You've Got to Hide Your Love Away.
_____00699581 Book/CD Pack...........................$12.95

VOLUME 14 – BLUES ROCK
Blue on Black • Crossfire • Cross Road Blues (Crossroads) • The House Is Rockin' • La Grange • Move It on Over • Roadhouse Blues • Statesboro Blues.
_____00699582 Book/CD Pack...........................$14.95

VOLUME 15 – R&B
Ain't Too Proud to Beg • Brick House • Get Ready • I Can't Help Myself (Sugar Pie, Honey Bunch) • I Got You (I Feel Good) • I Heard It Through the Grapevine • My Girl • Shining Star.
_____00699583 Book/CD Pack...........................$12.95

VOLUME 16 – JAZZ
All Blues • Black Orpheus • Bluesette • Footprints • Misty • Satin Doll • Stella by Starlight • Tenor Madness.
_____00699584 Book/CD Pack...........................$12.95

VOLUME 17 – COUNTRY
All My Rowdy Friends Are Coming over Tonight • Amie • Boot Scootin' Boogie • Chattahoochee • Folsom Prison Blues • Friends in Low Places • T-R-O-U-B-L-E • Workin' Man Blues.
_____00699588 Book/CD Pack...........................$12.95

VOLUME 18 – ACOUSTIC ROCK
About a Girl • Breaking the Girl • Drive • Iris • More Than Words • Patience • Silent Lucidity • 3 AM.
_____00699577 Book/CD Pack...........................$14.95

VOLUME 19 – SOUL
Get up (I Feel like Being) a Sex Machine • Green Onions • In the Midnight Hour • Knock on Wood • Mustang Sally • (Sittin' On) the Dock of the Bay • Soul Man • Walkin' the Dog.
_____00699578 Book/CD Pack...........................$12.95

VOLUME 20 – ROCKABILLY
Blue Suede Shoes • Bluejean Bop • Hello Mary Lou • Little Sister • Mystery Train • Rock This Town • Stray Cat Strut • That'll Be the Day.
_____00699580 Book/CD Pack...........................$12.95

VOLUME 21 – YULETIDE GUITAR PLAY-ALONG
Angels We Have Heard on High • Away in a Manger • Deck the Hall • The First Noel • Go, Tell It on the Mountain • Jingle Bells • Joy to the World • O Little Town of Bethlehem.
_____00699602 Book/CD Pack...........................$12.95

VOLUME 22 – CHRISTMAS GUITAR PLAY-ALONG
The Christmas Song (Chestnuts Roasting on an Open Fire) • Frosty the Snow Man • Happy Xmas (War Is Over) • Here Comes Santa Claus (Right down Santa Claus Lane) • Jingle-Bell Rock • Merry Christmas, Darling • Rudolph the Red-Nosed Reindeer • Silver Bells.
_____00699600 Book/CD Pack...........................$12.95

Prices, contents, and availability subject to change without notice.

FOR MORE INFORMATION, SEE YOUR LOCAL MUSIC DEALER, OR WRITE TO:

HAL•LEONARD®
CORPORATION
7777 W. BLUEMOUND RD. P.O. BOX 13819 MILWAUKEE, WI 53213

Visit Hal Leonard online at www.halleonard.com

0304

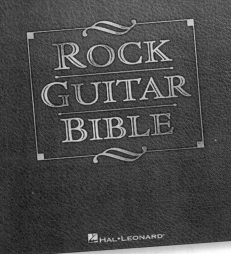

GUITAR BIBLES

from
HAL•LEONARD®

Hal Leonard proudly presents the Guitar Bible series. Each volume contains great songs in authentic, note-for-note transcriptions with lyrics and tablature.

ACOUSTIC GUITAR BIBLE
35 acoustic classics: Angie • Building a Mystery • Change the World • Dust in the Wind • Here Comes the Sun • Hold My Hand • Iris • Maggie May • Southern Cross • Tears in Heaven • Wild World • You Were Meant for Me • and more.
_____00690432....................................$19.95

ACOUSTIC ROCK GUITAR BIBLE
35 classics: About a Girl • And I Love Her • Behind Blue Eyes • Come to My Window • Crazy Little Thing Called Love • Free Fallin' • Give a Little Bit • If You Could Only See • More Than Words • Name • Night Moves • Not Fade Away • Pink Houses • Slide • Suite Madame Blue • Sweet Jane • 3 AM • and more.
_____00690625....................................$19.95

BABY BOOMER'S GUITAR BIBLE
35 songs: Angie • Can't Buy Me Love • Happy Together • Hey Jude • Imagine • Laughing • Longer • My Girl • New Kid in Town • Rebel, Rebel • Wild Thing • and more.
_____00690412....................................$19.95

BLUES GUITAR BIBLE
35 blues tunes: Boom Boom • Everyday (I Have the Blues) • Hide Away • I Can't Quit You Baby • I'm Your Hoochie Coochie Man • Killing Floor • Pride and Joy • Sweet Little Angel • The Thrill Is Gone • and more.
_____00690437....................................$19.95

BLUES-ROCK GUITAR BIBLE
35 songs: Cross Road Blues (Crossroads) • Hide Away • The House Is Rockin' • Love Struck Baby • Move It On Over • Piece of My Heart • Statesboro Blues • You Shook Me • more.
_____00690450....................................$19.95

COUNTRY GUITAR BIBLE
35 country classics: Ain't Goin' Down ('Til the Sun Comes Up) • Blue Eyes Crying in the Rain • Boot Scootin' Boogie • Friends in Low Places • I'm So Lonesome I Could Cry • T-R-O-U-B-L-E • and more.
_____00690465....................................$19.95

FOLK-ROCK GUITAR BIBLE
35 songs: At Seventeen • Blackbird • Fire and Rain • Happy Together • Leaving on a Jet Plane • Our House • Time in a Bottle • Turn! Turn! Turn! • You've Got a Friend • more.
_____00690464....................................$19.95

GRUNGE GUITAR BIBLE
30 songs: All Apologies • Counting Blue Cars • Glycerine • Hey Man Nice Shot • I'll Stick Around • Jesus Christ Pose • Lithium • Lump • Machinehead • Man in the Box • Molly (Sixteen Candles) • Nearly Lost You • Santa Monica • Seether • Smells like Teen Spirit • Song 2 • This Is a Call • Violet • Would? • and more.
_____00690649....................................$17.95

HARD ROCK GUITAR BIBLE
35 songs: Ballroom Blitz • Bang a Gong • Barracuda • Living After Midnight • Rock You like a Hurricane • School's Out • Welcome to the Jungle • You Give Love a Bad Name • more.
_____00690453....................................$19.95

INSTRUMENTAL GUITAR BIBLE
37 great instrumentals: Always with Me, Always with You • Big Foot • The Claw • Cliffs of Dover • For the Love of God • Frankenstein • Freeway Jam • Green Onions • Hide Away • Jessica • Lenny • Linus and Lucy • Perfidia • Pipeline • Raunchy • Rawhide • Rebel 'Rouser • Rumble • Satch Boogie • Scuttle Buttin' • Sleepwalk • The Stumble • T-Bone Shuffle • Tequila • Walk Don't Run • Wham • and more.
_____00690514....................................$19.95

JAZZ GUITAR BIBLE
31 songs: Body and Soul • In a Sentimental Mood • My Funny Valentine • Nuages • Satin Doll • So What • Star Dust • Take Five • Tangerine • Yardbird Suite • and more.
_____00690466....................................$19.95

NU METAL GUITAR BIBLE
25 edgy metal hits: Aenema • Black • Edgecrusher • Last Resort • People of the Sun • Schism • Sleep Now in the Fire • Southtown • Take a Look Around • Toxicity • Your Disease • Youth of the Nation • and more.
_____00690569....................................$19.95

POP/ROCK GUITAR BIBLE
35 pop hits: Change the World • Heartache Tonight • Hold My Hand • Money for Nothing • Mony, Mony • More Than Words • Pink Houses • Smooth • Summer of '69 • 3 AM • What I Like About You • and more.
_____00690517....................................$19.95

R&B GUITAR BIBLE
35 R&B classics: Brick House • Fire • I Got You (I Feel Good) • Love Rollercoaster • Shining Star • Sir Duke • Super Freak • and more.
_____00690452....................................$19.95

ROCK GUITAR BIBLE
33 songs: All Day and All of the Night • Born to Be Wild • Day Tripper • Gloria • Hey Joe • Jailhouse Rock • Money • Paranoid • Sultans of Swing • Walk This Way • You Really Got Me • more!
_____00690313....................................$19.95

ROCKABILLY GUITAR BIBLE
31 songs from artists such as Elvis, Buddy Holly and the Brian Setzer Orchestra: Blue Suede Shoes • Hello Mary Lou • Peggy Sue • Rock This Town • Travelin' Man • and more.
_____00690570....................................$17.95

SOUL GUITAR BIBLE
33 songs: Groovin' • I've Been Loving You Too Long • Let's Get It On • My Girl • Respect • Theme from Shaft • Soul Man • and more.
_____00690506....................................$19.95